影像中国

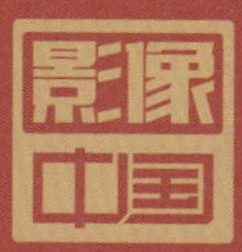

上海地标

Shanghai Landmarks

2017

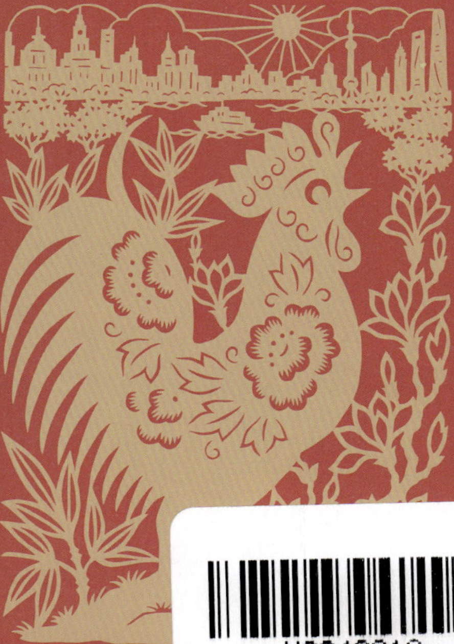

U0949219

中国出版集团 东方出版中心

影像·中国
上海地标
2017

壹
January
月

东方明珠电视塔
Oriental Pearl Radio & TV Tower

浦东新区世纪大道 1 号
No.1 Century Avenue, Pudong New Area

每年元旦举行登高迎新跑

高 468 米，集广播电视发射、观光、餐饮、购物、娱乐、游船、会展、历史陈列等多功能于一体。3 个 360 度的观光层让游客在不同的高度欣赏都市美景。国家 5A 景区。

With a height of 468 meters, the tower has mixed functions, including radio & TV transmission, sightseeing, catering, shopping, recreation, cruise tour, convention & exhibition, and historical displays. It has three 360-degree sightseeing floors that allow tourists to appreciate the charming metropolitan landscape at different heights. It is a 5A-rated national tourist attraction.

JAN. 1. 2017 SUNDAY

2017.1

农历丙申年腊月

1

初四　周日

元旦

环球金融中心
World Financial Center

浦东新区世纪大道 100 号
100 Century Avenue, Pudong New Area

新年登高揽胜绝佳处

与东方明珠、金茂大厦一起，形成上海新地标。楼高 492 米，是世界最高的平顶式大楼，其观光厅让人犹如置身云端。国家 4A 景区。

Shanghai World Financial Center (SWFC), together with the Oriental Pearl Radio & TV Tower and Jin Mao Tower, are new landmarks of Shanghai. A height of 492 meters makes it the tallest flat-roof building in the world. You will feel like being surrounded by clouds while standing on its observatory. It is a 4A-rated national tourist attraction.

2

初五　周一

中华艺术宫
China Art Museum

浦东新区上南路 205 号
205 Shangnan Road, Pudong New Area

由世博会中国馆改建而成，其前身上海美术馆是新中国最早建立的美术馆之一。收藏美术精品，开展学术研究、举办陈列展览、普及审美教育等。

The museum is renovated from China Pavilion of Expo. Its predecessor is the Shanghai Art Museum, one of the earliest art museums since the foundations of the People's Republic of China. The museum is dedicated to collecting exquisite art works, conducting academic study, holding exhibitions and popularizing esthetic education, etc.

JAN. 3. 2017 TUESDAY

2017.1

农历丙申年腊月

3

初六　周二

磁悬浮列车

Maglev Train

浦东新区龙阳路 2100 号
2100 Longyang Road, Pudong New Area

2003 年 1 月 4 日正式运营

世界第一条磁悬浮商运专线，中德合作开发，2003 年初正式投运，连接龙阳路地铁站和浦东国际机场。专线全长 29.863 公里，全程仅需 8 分钟。

It is the first commercially operated magnetic levitation line in the world, jointly developed by China and Germany. It was put into operation officially in early 2003, and connects Longyang Subway Station and Pudong International Airport. The line has a total length of 29.863km. It only takes 8 minutes to finish the whole journey.

JAN. 4. 2017 WEDNESDAY

2017.1

农历丙申年腊月

4

初七　周三

徐家汇源
Xujiahui Origin

徐家汇地区
in the Xujiahui region

集历史建筑、宗教、文化、教育等多个方面为一体的综合人文景区。景区内有徐家汇天主堂、徐家汇观象台、徐家汇藏书楼等文物保护建筑，享有“启蒙之光”、“海派之源”、“时尚之汇”之誉。国家 4A 景区。

It is a comprehensive cultural attraction with such elements as historical architecture, religion, culture and education. There are historical buildings under protection in this area including the Xujiahui Catholic Church, Observatory, and Library, all of which, as it were, have contributed to its reputations as “Light of Enlightenment”, “Origin of Shanghai Culture (Haipai)”, and “Fashion Center”. It is a 4A-rated national tourist attraction.

5

初八　周四

腊八节　小寒

辰山植物园
Chenshan Botanical Garden

松江区辰花公路 3888 号
3888 Chenhua Highway, Songjiang District

华东地区规模最大的植物园。集科研、科普和观赏游览于一体，收集植物约 9000 种，是华东区系植物最多的综合植物园。国家 4A 景区。

As the largest botanical garden in Eastern China, it boasts an integration of functions such as scientific research, science promotion and tourism, and collects about 9,000 species of plants, which makes it a comprehensive botanical garden with the most species of plants of Eastern China. It is a 4A-rated national tourist attraction.

6

初九　周五

淮海路

Huaihai Road

黄浦区
in Huangpu District

上海最繁华的商业街之一，旧时谓霞飞路。与南京东路相比，淮海路的商业层次高端，街区更多地留存了旧时法租界的风格和情调。

It is one of the most prosperous shopping streets in Shanghai, formerly known as Avenue Joffre in old times. Compared with Nanjing Road, Huaihai Road is more upscale, and features a galaxy of talented people, abundant connotation and exotic atmosphere.

7

初十　周六

南翔老街

Nanxiang Old Street

嘉定区南翔镇
in Nanxiang Town, Jiading District

一条较为纯粹地保留了清末民初“银南翔”历史风貌的古街道，粉墙黛瓦，屋舍、商铺鳞次栉比；小桥、流水、花园、长廊、画店林林总总，各具风韵。国家 4A 景区。

It is an old street that has purely retained the historical appearance of “Silver Nanxiang” in the late Qing Dynasty and early Republic period, with a charming array of pink walls, dark tiles, homes, stores, small bridges, running waters, gardens, corridors, and painting stores. It is a 4A-rated national tourist attraction.

JAN. 8. 2017 SUNDAY

2017.1

农历丙申年腊月

8

十一　周日

华业公寓（华业大楼）

Huaye Apartment (Huaye Building)

静安区陕西北路 175 弄
Lane 175 North Shaanxi Road, Jing'an District

建于 1934 年，由上海营造巨商谭干臣投资兴建、李锦沛设计的西班牙式风格建筑，属折衷主义向现代建筑过度时期的作品，旧时住户多为沪上闻人。市级文物保护单位。

As a heritage site under municipal protection, it is a Spanish-style structure built by Tan Qianchen, and designed by Li Jinpei, the giant construction merchants in Shanghai in 1934.

9

十二　周一

大新公司（第一百货商店）

Da Hsin Company (No. 1 Department Store)

黄浦区南京东路 830 号
830 East Nanjing Road, Huangpu District

1936 年 1 月 10 日开业

旧上海百货四大公司之一，上海老字号，是矗立在上海闹市中心的一幢浅黄色瓷砖贴面、外观为装饰艺术派风格的十层大厦。现为上海市第一百货商店。市级文物保护单位。

As one of the four major department stores in Shanghai before 1949, Da Hsin Company is also the largest department store in China and a Shanghai Time-honored Brand. It is a historical and cultural site protected at the municipal level.

10

十三　周二

兰心大戏院

Lyceum Theatre

黄浦区茂名路 57 号
No. 57, Maoming Road, Huangpu District

中国最早的欧洲式剧场，上海历史最久的剧场之一，清同治年间由英侨集资创建，典雅欧式建筑风格。光绪年间曾公演话剧《黑奴吁天录》。近年投巨资修建。上海优秀历史建筑。

As the earliest European-style theatre in China and one of the oldest theatres in Shanghai, it was built with the funds offered by British Chinese in the period reigned by the Tongzhi Emperor of the Qing Dynasty. It features the elegant European architectural style. In the period reigned by the Guangxu Emperor, the drama Uncle Tom's Cabin was staged here. It has seen rebuilding in recent years with huge funds and is regarded as an excellent historical architecture in Shanghai.

11

十四　周三

法善庵

Fa Shan Nunnery

杨浦区政本路 338 号
338 Zhengben Road, Yangpu District

民俗腊月十五吃素日

始建于清朝末年的尼姑庵。1996 年底修复。主要建筑有大雄宝殿、伽蓝殿、念佛堂、藏经阁等，飞角重檐，结构雄伟，庵貌庄严肃静。

Fa Shan Nunnery, formerly a Buddhist nunnery built at the end of the Qing Dynasty, enjoys a long standing reputation and is frequently visited by visitors. It was renovated at the end of 1996. The main buildings include the Grand Hall, the Hall of Dharma Protectors, Recitation Hall, and Sutra Collection Pavilion. It features the double-eaved roof, majestic structure, dignified Buddha statues and solemn and silent ambience.

12

十五 周四

方塔园
Fang Ta Park

松江区中山东路 235 号
235 East Zhongshan Road, Songjiang District

松江古城中一座以观赏历史文物为主体的园林。园内方塔、照壁为全国少见的至今保护较好的精美古建筑，均为全国重点文物保护单位。国家 4A 景区。

It is a park in the ancient town of Songjiang featuring historical and cultural relics. The square pagoda and screen wall in it are the few exquisite ancient structures that have been kept intact in the whole country. Both are Major Historical and Cultural Sites Protected at the National Level. Fang Ta Park is a 4A-rated national tourist attraction in China.

13

十六　周五

南京路

Nanjing Road

黄浦区
in Huangpu District

上海开埠后最早建立的一条商业街。南京东路主要是平价商业区和旅游区；南京西路则是全上海最高端的时尚商业观光街区。

It is one of the earliest business streets established after the opening of Shanghai to the world. East Nanjing Road is a fair-price commercial zone and tourist area, while West Nanjing Road is the most luxurious and fashionable commercial zone in Shanghai, with a focus on luxury goods and high-end personalized consumption.

JAN. 14. 2017 SATURDAY

2017.1

农历丙申年腊月

14

十七　周六

雍福会
YongFoo Elite

徐汇区永福路 200 号
200 Yongfu Road, Xuhui District

上世纪初建造的欧式风格建筑。1980 年后为英国领事馆，现为高档会所，胡润百富榜“最受青睐的上海顶级俱乐部”第一名。

YongFoo Elite is a European style building completed at the beginning of the last century. It became a British Consulate after 1980. Now it is a luxury clubhouse of Shanghai's rich circles and ranks the first in the “Most Popular Top-grade Clubs of Shanghai” of Hurun Rich List.

JAN. 15. 2017 SUNDAY

2017.1

农历丙申年腊月

15

十八　周日

红房子西餐厅
Maison Pourcel

黄浦区淮海中路 845 号
845 Middle Huaihai Road, Huangpu District

红房子西餐厅是上海滩最悠久的品牌法式西菜馆，是许多老上海人接触西餐的发源地，由孪生兄弟、米其林星级厨师 Jacques 和 Laurent Pourcel 创立。就餐氛围为法式的浪漫情调。

Established by twin brothers Jacques and Laurent Pourcel, the Red House Restaurant is the most time-honored French-style Western Restaurant in Shanghai and where many old Shanghainese got to know the western style foods. The restaurant is filled with French-style romantic atmosphere.

16

十九　周一

法华塔

Fahua Pagoda

嘉定区南大街 349 号
349 South street, Jiading District

冬季赏雪佳处

始建于南宋开禧年间，是嘉定设县的源点，因塔内存有一部《法华经》而得名。又俗名文笔峰，有祈求科举中式之意，被视为嘉定文风之所赖。市级文物保护单位。

This pagoda was built during Kaixi Period of the Southern Song Dynasty. It is the original point of Jiading County and gains its name from the Lotus Sutra (Fahua Sutra) stored inside. Hence the pagoda was deemed as the foundation of the literary style of Jiading. It is a historical and cultural site protected at the municipal level.

17

二十 周二

静安“金三角”
“Golden Triangle” in Jing’an

静安区
in Jing'an District

2007 年 1 月 18 日 “金三角”整体成形

以聚集在南京西路、陕西路口附近的恒隆广场、梅龙镇广场和中信泰富等三座国际甲级商厦为标志的“上海第一商圈”，汇聚大量世界一线品牌、国际顶级精品的专卖店、旗舰店。

It is Shanghai’s No. 1 business center relying on such international Grade A buildings as Plaza 66, Westgate Mall and CITIC Square, and gathers a number of franchised stores and flagship stores of the world’s first-class brands and international top quality goods in Shanghai.

JAN. 18. 2017 WEDNESDAY　　*2017.1*　　农历丙申年腊月

18

廿一　周三

大上海大戏院（大上海电影院）

Shanghai Grand Theatre (Shanghai Grand Cinema)

黄浦区西藏中路 500 号
500 Middle Xizang Road, Huangpu District

1933 年所建的标准五星级电影院。建筑华丽，设施现代，时人谓可与大光明媲美，现代主义风格。夜间大门上方八根霓虹灯玻璃方柱为其形象标识。市级文物保护单位。

This standard five-star cinema was built in 1933. Its gorgeous building with modern facilities can be comparable with the Grand Theatre. It is a heritage site under municipal protection.

19

廿二 周四

外白渡桥
Garden Bridge

黄浦区中山东一路黄浦公园旁
Near Huangpu Park, No.1 East Zhongshan Road, Huangpu District

1908 年 1 月 20 日通车

中国第一座全钢结构铆接桥梁和仅存的不等高桁架结构桥。自 1908 年落成通车，一直是上海现代化和工业化的象征。现为上海市优秀历史建筑。

It is China's first riveted bridge of all-steel structure and one of a few bridges with unequal height truss. Since it was open to traffic in 1908, the bridge has been a symbol of modernization and industrialization of Shanghai. Now it has been rated as one of Shanghai's excellent historical buildings.

20

廿三　周五

小年　大寒

800 秀创意园
800 SHOW Creative Park

静安区常德路 800 号
800 Changde Road, Jing'an District

集休闲、展览、办公于一体的花园式创意产业园。园内建筑及整体设计中西合璧、新旧交融，吸引了众多文化创意机构入驻，上海市文化创意产业推进领导小组办公室在此办公。

Being a garden style culture innovation base and a multi-functional territory combined leisure, exhibition and official business as one, with the overall design and construct concept conceives both Chinese and Western elements, it attracts a series of cultural investors and vendors, as well as the lead team office of SHCCI-ministry in charge of promoting Shanghai's cultural and creative industries, to station here.

JAN. 21. 2017 SATURDAY

2017.1

农历丙申年腊月

21

廿四　周六

四川北路商业街

North Sichuan Road Business Street

虹口区
in Hongkou District

民国以来上海最为繁华商业街之一。上世纪 90 年代至今，被认为是仅次于南京路和淮海路的上海第三大商业街，形成“南繁、中专、北雅”的商业格局。

It is one of the busiest business streets in Shanghai since the Republic of China. Since 1990s, it has been considered as the third largest business street only next to Nanjing Road and Huaihai Road. Now it has formed the new business layout of “Prosperous in the south, dedicated in the middle and elegant in the north”.

JAN. 22. 2017 SUNDAY

2017.1

农历丙申年腊月

22

廿五　周日

新新公司（第一食品商店）

Sun Sun Company (First Food Hall)

黄浦区南京东路 720 号
720 East Nanjing Road, Huangpu District

1926 年 1 月 23 日开业

旧上海四大百货公司之一，上海老字号，名号寓意“日新又新”。建成于 1926 年，坐北朝南，折衷主义风格。目前建筑使用单位是上海市第一食品商店。市级文物保护单位。

Built in 1926, the building of Sun Sun Company, one of the four major department stores in Shanghai before 1949 and a Shanghai Time-honored Brand, boasts a distinctive architectural pattern. It is a historical and cultural site protected at the municipal level.

23

廿六 周一

静安雕塑公园

Jing'an Sculpture Park

静安区石门二路 128 号
128 Shimen Road Number Two, Jing'an District

中心城区公园绿地与文化设施结合的成功范例，兼具生态功能、艺术功能、文化功能的开放式城市公园。除一系列现代艺术雕塑外，公园植物有申城首次引进的珍贵红叶石楠、常绿萱草等。

Jing'an Sculpture Park is an open urban park with integrated functions of ecology, art and culture, as well as a model for the integration of public parks and cultural facilities in the downtown. The park features the precious Photinia fraseri and Hemerocallis sempervirens Araki that Shanghai introduced for the first time.

24

廿七　周二

城隍庙
City God Temple

黄浦区方浜中路 249 号
249 Middle Fangbang Road, Huangpu District

坐落于豫园旅游景区，是上海地区重要的道教宫观。始建于三国，明永乐年间改建为城隍庙。前殿祭祀金山神霍光，正殿供城隍神秦裕伯。全国重点文物保护单位。

Located in the tourist spots of Yu Garden, the City God Temple of Shanghai is an important Taoist temple in Shanghai. It is a historical and cultural site protected at both national and municipal level.

JAN. 25. 2017 WEDNESDAY　　*2017.1*　　农历丙申年腊月

25

廿八　周三

汾阳路 45 号住宅（海关专科学校）

Residence at No.45 Fenyang Road (Customs College)

徐汇区汾阳路 45 号
45 Fenyang Road, Xuhui District

1 月 26 日国际海关日

西班牙建筑风格的独立式两层楼花园住宅，富蕴欧式建筑宁静和高贵气质，建于 1932 年，曾是首位执掌海关领导权的中国人丁贵堂的寓所。市级文物保护单位。

This two-story free-standing garden house of Spanish architectural style was built in 1932, and was once the residence of Ding Guitang, the first Chinese in charge of customs. It is a heritage site under municipal protection.

26

廿九　周四

宋庆龄故居纪念馆

Soong Ching Ling Memorial Residence

徐汇区淮海中路 1843 号
1843 Middle Huaihai Road, Xuhui District

1893 年 1 月 27 日宋庆龄诞辰

宋庆龄女士生前在沪寓所原址上建立的人文类纪念馆。展陈手稿、信函、照片、生活用品等珍贵文物 1.3 万余件。国家 4A 级旅游景区、全国重点文物保护单位。

It is a cultural memorial built on the former residence of Ms. Soong Ching Ling in Shanghai. It displays more than 13,000 pieces of precious cultural relics, such as manuscripts, letters, photos and living articles. It is a 4A-rated national tourist attraction and one of the Major Historical and Cultural Sites Protected at the National Level.

27

三十 周五

除夕

豫园
Yu Garden

黄浦区安仁街 132 号
132 Anren Street, Huangpu District

豫园灯会正月初一到十八

上海老城厢仅存的明代园林，被称为“上海的根”，是上海特有的人文标志和文化名片。作为“全国四大文化市场”之一，与潘家园、琉璃厂、夫子庙齐名。国家 4A 景区。

Being the only garden of the Ming Dynasty that survives in the old town of Shanghai, the Yu Garden, seen as the “Root of Shanghai”, is a unique symbol of the culture of Shanghai. The Yu Garden shares a reputation as one of the “four cultural markets in China” with Panjiayuan, Liulichang, and Fuzimiao. It is a 4A-rated national tourist attraction.

JAN. 28. 2017 SATURDAY

2017.1

农历丁酉年正月

28

初一　周六

春节

金茂大厦
Jin Mao Tower

世纪大道 88 号
88 Century Avenue, Pudong New Area

新年登高揽胜绝佳处

高 420.5 米，融汇中西方建筑艺术的智慧型摩天大楼，海派建筑的里程碑。大厦 88 层观光厅，是目前国内最高最大的观光厅，上海大世界基尼斯之最。国家 5A 景区。

It is a 420.5-meter smart skyscraper combining both Chinese and Western architectural arts. The observation deck on the 88th floor is currently the highest and largest one in China, according to the records of Shanghai Great World Guinness. It is a 5A-rated national tourist attraction.

JAN. 29. 2017 SUNDAY

2017.1

农历丁酉年正月

29

初二　周日

上海外滩历史文化街区

Historical Conservation Block of the Bund

黄浦区中山东一路
No.1 East Zhongshan Road, Shanghai

第一次鸦片战争后上海设立租界。这里是租界时代上海的金融中心、外贸机构的集中带，是百年上海的标志性建筑和象征，有“万国建筑博览”之称。全国重点文物保护单位。

It is the financial center of Shanghai and the aggregation belt of foreign trade firms in the era of concessions. They are also the iconic buildings and a symbol of Shanghai in the recent one hundred years, and known as the “Expo of Buildings”. It is an important heritage site under state protection.

30

初三　周一

文庙
Confucian Temple

黄浦区文庙路 215 号
215 Wenmiao Road, Huangpu District

春节祈福热门地之一

上海市区唯一的一座祭祀孔子的庙学合一的古建筑群。始建于元代，在近代是旧城厢的文化中心。市级文物保护单位。

As the highest learning institution of Shanghai before the Republic of China was established, it is the sole ancient building complex to worship Confucius and integrates the functions of both temple and school. It is now a municipality protected historic and cultural site.

31

初四 周二

影像·中国
上海地标
2017

贰
February
月

锦江乐园

Jinjiang Action Park

闵行区虹梅路 201 号
201 Hongmei Road, Minhang District

1985 年 2 月 1 日开业

20 世纪 80 年代通过引进国外游乐设施建造的上海第一家大型游乐园。分“陆上世界”和“水上世界”两大部分，有 40 多项游乐项目，营运至今，适合各种年龄游客游玩。国家 4A 景区。

It is the first large amusement park in Shanghai built through the introduction of foreign amusement facilities in 1980s. It is made up of a “Land World” and an “Aquatic World” that offer over 40 amusement projects suitable for visitors of different age groups. It is a 4A-rated national tourist attraction.

1

初五　周三

新江湾城湿地公园

New Jiangwan City Wetland Park

杨浦区殷行路 880 号
880 Yinhang Road, Yangpu District

2 月 2 日世界湿地日

原系江湾军用机场旧址，由于长期停用，林灌型、森林型、湿地型、农田型的生态环境纷纷复出，成为市区唯一一块自然生态“绿宝石”，被列入上海未来 4 大示范居住区。

It was formerly the Jiangwan Military Airport. As the airport has not been in service for a long time, the ecological environment of shrub, forest, wetland and farmland reappeared. Therefore, this park has been the only one "emerald" of natural ecology in the downtown, and has been included into Shanghai's four major demonstration residential areas of the future.

2

初六 周四

世界湿地日

嘉里中心

Jing An Kerry Centre

静安区南京西路 1515 号
1515 West Nanjing Road, Jing'an District

毗邻上海展览中心，以优越的位置和新颖的设计概念，满足商务和居住的要求。各国领事馆、银行、跨国企业、高级餐厅近在咫尺。

Located on Nanjing Road of Jing'an District with row upon row of shops, it borders on Shanghai Exhibition Center and meets the requirements for both business and residence on the strength of its superior location and novel design concept. Consulates of all countries, banks, transnational enterprises and high-level restaurants are around the corner.

FEB. 3. 2017 FRIDAY

2017.2

农历丁酉年正月

3

初七　周五

立春

上海中心大厦
Shanghai Tower

浦东新区银城中路 501 号
501 Middle Yincheng Road, Pudong New Area

上海中心大厦高 632 米，是中国第二、世界第三超高层建筑。大厦以办公为主，其他业态有会展、酒店、观光娱乐、商业等。

The 632 meter-tall Shanghai Tower is currently the tallest building in Shanghai, and forms a rising arc together with Jin Mao Tower and the Shanghai World Financial Center. Dedicated to office, the Shanghai Tower also includes other commercial formats such as convention & exhibition, hotel, sightseeing & recreation and business.

FEB. 4. 2017 SATURDAY

2017.2

农历丁酉年正月

4

初八　周六

安亭老街

Anting Old Street

嘉定区安亭镇安亭街（近新源路）
Anting Street, Anting Town, Jiading District (near Xinyuan Road)

历史悠久，文化底蕴深厚，呈江南水乡“路—桥—街”格局，具明清韵味的繁华老街。主要有严泗桥、菩提寺、震川书院等古迹，及 F1 赛车场、汽车博物馆等现代景点。

With a long history and profound cultural deposits, it is a prosperous old street with the flavor of Ming and Qing Dynasties. It boasts not only historical sites such as Yansi Bridge, Puti Temple, Zhenchuan Academy of Classical Learning, but also modern scenic spots such as F1 Racing Circuit and Automotive Museum.

FEB. 5. 2017 SUNDAY

2017.2

农历丁酉年正月

5

初九　周日

滨江大道
Riverside Promenade

浦东新区
Pudong New Area

黄浦江东堤岸的一条有亲水平台的观光人行大道，与浦西外滩隔江相望，1997 年建成，全长 2500 米，由景观道路等组成，被称为浦东的新外滩。

Riverside Promenade is a promenade with touching-water platform along the eastern bank of the Huangpu River and faces the Bund to its west. Completed in 1997, and with a total length of 2,500 meters made up of sightseeing routes, it is reputed as the New Bund of Pudong.

6

初十　周一

黄浦饭店

Huangpu Hotel

虹口区黄浦路 15 号
15 Huangpu Road, Hongkou District

坐落于浏览浦江全景的最佳观赏点——外白渡桥桥堍旁，被海内外誉为景观资源绝佳的观景酒店。步行可至外滩观景区、南京东路。

Located at one end of Garden Bridge - the best position for the full view of the Huangpu River, it is reputed as a viewing platform with excellent landscape resources. It is within walking distance to Lookout Area of the Bund, East Nanjing Road.

FEB. 7. 2017 TUESDAY

2017.2

农历丁酉年正月

7

十一　周二

淞沪抗战纪念馆
Songhu War Memorial

宝山区友谊路 1 号
No. 1 Youyi Road, Baoshan District

位于两次淞沪抗战的主战场，主体建筑是一座纪念塔，二层展区陈列了大量珍贵文物。顶层设观景台，可远眺长江口、俯瞰宝山城。有大型雕塑、主题墙。国家三级博物馆。

It was the main battlefield of the two Songhu battles. Now there is a monument which is the main building and a large number of precious cultural relics in the two-story exhibition hall. It is a Grade-Three national museum.

FEB. 8. 2017 WEDNESDAY

2017.2

农历丁酉年正月

8

十二　周三

广富林遗址

Guangfulin Historical and Cultural Site

松江区方松街道广富林路
Guangfulin Road, Fangsong Sub-district, Songjiang District

正月初一至正月十五免费参观

新石器时代松江的原住民与4000年前来自黄河流域的最早一批移民共同创造的上海古文化“根系”，增补了上海古文化文明的组成系列。全国重点文物保护单位。

It is the “root” of ancient Shanghai culture created jointly by the locals of Songjiang in the Neolithic Age and the earliest immigrants from the Yellow River basin 4,000 years ago, which further diversified the ancient cultural civilization of Shanghai. It is an important heritage site under state protection.

9

十三　周四

金城银行大楼（交通银行）

Kincheng Banking Corp. Mansion (Bank of Communications)

黄浦区江西中路 200 号
200 Middle Jiangxi Road, Huangpu District

1924 年由华资“北四行”支柱金城银行投建、近代著名建筑师庄俊与赍丰洋行联合设计的总部大楼。钢筋混凝土框架结构，英国新古典派道维克式立面。市级文物保护单位。

This is an office building designed by the first generation of architects of China in 1924, and among the most luxurious buildings of Chinese-invested banks. It is a heritage site under municipal protection. The lintels and other locals are of baroque decoration, and the entire building integrates the neoclassical eclectic style.

FEB. 10. 2017 FRIDAY

2017.2

农历丁酉年正月

10

十四　周五

玉佛寺

Yufo Temple

普陀区安远路 170 号
170 Anyuan Road, Putuo District

玉佛寺礼佛香期正月十五，春秋最佳

建于 1918 年的沪上名刹，因寺内的两尊玉佛而得名并闻名遐迩。地处繁华闹市，却闹中取静，被喻为闹市中的一片净土。寺庙师承宋代寺院风格，布局整齐，结构精巧，金碧辉煌。

As a famous temple built in 1918, it is well-known far and wide for two jade Buddhas. Located in lively bustling streets, this Temple keeps quiet in a noisy neighborhood, so it is rated as a pure land in the noisy city. Following the style of temples of Song Dynasty, the temple is in tidy layout, ingenious structure and majestic decoration.

FEB. 11. 2017 SATURDAY

2017.2

农历丁酉年正月

11

十五　周六

元宵节

朱家角古镇

Zhujiajiao Ancient Town

青浦区朱家角镇
Zhujiajiao Town, Qingpu District

发轫于三国时期的千年古镇，历史悠久，底蕴深厚.已开放了课植园、城隍庙、大清邮局等20多个景点。上海市四大古镇之一、国家4A景区。

With a history of around 1,000 years dating back to the Three Kingdoms Period, it is an ancient town with profundity. Currently over 20 attractions are open to the public, including Kezhi Garden, the City God's Temple, and the Post Office of the Qing Dynasty. It is one of the four major ancient towns in Shanghai and one of the 4A-rated national tourist attractions in China.

FEB. 12. 2017 SUNDAY

2017.2

农历丁酉年正月

12

十六　周日

翰林匾额博物馆

Museum of Horizontal Inscribed Boards in Academician Residences

青浦区朱家角镇东井街 122 号
122 Dongjing Street, Zhujiajiao Town, Qingpu District

收藏全国各地古代木制匾额 1060 方，创同类之最。馆藏分文人匾（进士以上）、官宦匾（二品以上）、重大家族堂号匾、民国要员匾 4 个主题。入上海非物质文化遗产保护名录。

The museum has a collection of 1,060 ancient wooden horizontal inscribed boards from all over the country, ranking the first among its kind. The collections are divided into four categories: boards in scholars' residences, boards in officials' residences, boards inscribed with name of ancestral hall of major families and boards of key officials' residences. The museum has been included into the List of Intangible Cultural Heritages in Shanghai.

FEB. 13. 2017 MONDAY

2017.2

农历丁酉年正月

13

十七　周一

甜爱路

Tian'ai Road

虹口区
in Hongkou District

上海最浪漫马路，前身为民国时期的公园靶子场路、千爱里（路）。抗战胜利后起谐音改称“甜爱路”。标志街景为情人墙、爱心邮局，是恋人甜蜜拥吻和刻字留念之处。

Tian'ai Road, the most romantic road in Shanghai, was formerly known as the Park Bazichang Road and Qian Ai Li (Road) in the Republic of China. After the victory of the Anti-Japanese War, it was renamed Tian'ai Road. Boasting iconic street scenes including Lovers Wall and Post Office of Love, it is a good place for lovers to hug and kiss each other.

FEB. 14. 2017 TUESDAY

2017.2

农历丁酉年正月

14

十八　周二

情人节

上海影城
Shanghai Film Art Center

长宁区新华路 160 号
160 Xinhua Road, Changning District

沪上首家五星级影院，1991 年建成，是历届上海国际电影节的主会场。共有 9 个风格迥异的电影放映厅，硬件设施领先全国同行。建成至今，党和国家领导人，众多的国内外明星都曾在此留下光影。

Established in 1991, Shanghai Film Art Center is the first five-star theater in Shanghai and the main venue of the Shanghai International Film Festival. It has 9 projection halls with different styles and its hardware facilities are believed to be at the forefront ofthe industry. Since its establishment, CPCand State leaders and lots of stars from home and abroad have come here and left their mark.

15

十九　周三

大公馆
Grand Hall

徐汇区东湖路 7 号
7 Donghu Road, Xuhui District

1925 年建造的法国文艺复兴式花园住宅。相传爱因斯坦访沪曾住，并一度成为杜月笙私宅的一部分。建国后曾为苏联驻华商务代表处上海分处的驻地。目前为东方财富股份有限公司使用。上海市优秀历史保护建筑。

It was a Renaissance-style garden house designed and built by a French designer in 1925. And its final owner was a Jewish businessman Hannah Joseph. After the founding of the People's Republic of China, it was once the base of the Shanghai Branch of Soviet Union's Office of Commercial Representatives in China. It's now an excellent historic preservation building in Shanghai.

16

二十 周四

1933 老场坊

1933 Old Millfun

虹口区溧阳路 611 号
611 Liyang Road,
Hongkou District

2008 年 2 月改建

前身旧上海工部局宰牲场。现为融时尚发布、工艺设计、品牌定制、创意休闲为一体的文化创意园区，汇聚了一批艺术家、设计师、教育家、企业精英和创始人，成为一个保持巴洛克风格的创意生活体验中心。

It is a creative life experience center of Baroque style, which integrates fashion release, creative design, brand customization, culture seeking and creation & leisure, and gathers together arts, design masters, educationalists and enterprise elites. Its predecessor is the abattoir of the former Shanghai Municipal Council.

FEB. 17. 2017 FRIDAY

2017.2

农历丁酉年正月

17

廿一　周五

龙音寺

Longyin Temple

闵行区闵东路 1 号(近南溪路)
1 Mindong Road(near Nanxi Road), Minhang District

1996 年 2 月修复

原名观音阁，始建于清朝乾隆年间，寺名取自观音来此白龙现身之意。三层重檐殿堂，底层设讲堂，二楼为大雄宝殿，三楼为藏经阁。现今香火旺盛，信众云集。

Formerly called Avalokitesvara Pavilion and built under the reign of Emperor Qianlong in the Qing Dynasty, the temple gets its name from the meaning that the Goddess of Mercy came to the temple and the white dragon appeared. The temple is a three-storey building, including the auditorium at the bottom, the great Buddha's hall on the second floor, and the depositary of Buddhist texts on the third floor. Nowadays, increasing faithful believers have gathered at the exuberant temple.

18

廿二　周六

雨水

绿波廊

Lvbolang Restaurant

黄浦区豫园路 115 号老城隍庙内
115 Yuyuan Road, the Old City God's Temple, Huangpu District

1973 年 2 月 19 日接待西哈努克亲王时形成“基因菜谱”

最具海派风情的餐馆老字号，始建于明嘉靖年间，以海派菜系的国宴、船点著称，以接待英国女皇、美国总统等世界政要、名流而享誉海内外。就餐环境幽雅，古色古香，具有浓郁的中国传统氛围。

Founded under the reign of Emperor Jiajing, it is a time-honored restaurant brand of Shanghai flavor. Offering well-known Shanghai-style state banquet and Suzhou-style desserts, the Hotel is reputed at home and abroad for receiving leaders and celebrities all over the world. The elegant and antique dining environment manifests rich Chinese traditional atmosphere.

19

廿三　周日

枫泾古镇
Fengjing Ancient Town

金山区枫泾镇
in Fengjing Town, Jinshan District

上海市第一个“中国历史文化名镇”。具有 1500 年历史，文化底蕴深厚，体现在建筑、宗教、饮食等各个方面，是上海地区现存规模较大、保存完好的水乡古镇。国家 4A 景区。

It is the first “famous historical and cultural town of China” in Shanghai. With a history of 1,500 years, it has a profound cultural foundation, which is reflected in architecture, religion, food and many other aspects. It is a large riverside ancient town well preserved in Shanghai and a 4A-rated national tourist attraction.

20

廿四　周一

马勒别墅

Moller Villa

黄浦区陕西南路 30 号
30 South Shaanxi Road,
Huangpu District

1936 年竣工，英籍犹太人马勒的私人花园别墅，中西方建筑完美融合，主建筑为三层斯堪的那维亚式挪威风格建筑，花园和楼内细部有中国味道。全国重点文物保护单位。

Completed in 1936, it was a private garden villa of an English Jew named Moller. It is a perfect combination of Chinese and Western architectural elements. The main structure is a three-story Scandinavian building of Norwegian style while details in the garden and within the building present a Chinese touch. It is an important heritage site under state protection.

FEB. 21. 2017 TUESDAY

2017.2

农历丁酉年正月

21

廿五　周二

席家花园总店

Xi's Garden Headquarters

徐汇区东平路 1 号
No.1 Dongping Road, Xuhui District

建于上世纪 20 年代的花园洋房。原为民国时中央造币厂厂长、宋子文同学席德柄的私邸。目前为沪上著名的以怀旧氛围和本帮菜肴为特色的连锁餐饮酒店。

Xi's Garden is a chain hotel featuring nostalgic ambience and local cuisine, whose first outlet is opened in a garden house built at 1 Dongping Road in the 1920s. It was formerly the private residence of Xi Debing, the Factory Director of the Central Mint during the Republic of China and a classmate of Song Ziwen.

22

廿六　周三

罗店古镇

Luodian Town

宝山区

in Baoshan District

正月灯会

具江南水乡风光及厚重人文内涵的历史古镇。始建于元代至正年间，元明清时宝山首镇。清初，棉花、棉布交易兴隆，故有金罗店之称。现有梵王宫、丰德桥等古代建筑。

This is an ancient town with natural landscape of the southern Yangtze River Delta and heavy cultural connotations. Founded in the ruling periods of Zhiyuan Emperor in the Ming Dynasty, Luodian became the first town in Baoshan District in the Qing Dynasty. The early days of the Qing Dynasty witnessed the booming trading of cotton and cotton, so the town was called "Golden Luodian" then. Now, there are Lord Brahma's Palace, Fengde Bridge and other ancient buildings.

23

廿七　周四

莘庄公园

Xinzhuang Park

闵行区莘浜路 421 号
421 Xinbang Road, Minhang District

2 月梅花展

由民国私家花园改扩建而来，以观赏梅花、樱花和桂花为特色的城市公园。公园以芙蓉潭为中心，沿潭设置亭、榭、假山，构成层次丰富多彩的景色。上海市五星级公园。

As Shanghai's five-star park, Xinzhuang Park arisen from a private garden during the period of the Republic of China, and is a city garden featuring plum, cherry and sweet-scented osmanthus.

24

廿八 周五

城市规划展示馆

Urban Planning Exhibition Center

黄浦区人民大道 100 号
100 People Avenue, Huangpu District

2000 年 2 月 25 日开馆

展示上海城市规划与建设成就的专业性场馆。坐落在人民广场和人民公园之间，是全面整体深入认识上海的观展选择。国家 4A 景区。

It's a professional venue that shows the achievements of urban planning and construction made by Shanghai. Its location between the People's Square and the People's Park makes it the best choice to get an overall, complete and clear understanding of Shanghai. It is a 4A-rated national tourist attraction.

25

廿九　周六

海洋水族馆
Ocean Aquarium

浦东新区陆家嘴环路 1388 号
1388 Lujiazui Ring Road,
Pudong New Area

2002 年 2 月建成开放

一座具有国际一流水准的现代化大型海洋水族馆，也是世界上最大的人造海水水族馆之一。内设九大展区，展出来自五大洲四大洋多种珍稀鱼类及稀有生物。国家 4A 景区。

It is a large state-of-the-art modern ocean aquarium of international standard and also one of the biggest artificial sea water aquariums in the world. The aquarium is made up of nine different zones that have a collection of rare fishes and rare wildlife from five continents and four oceans. It is a 4A-rated national tourist attraction.

FEB. 26. 2017 SUNDAY

2017.2

农历丁酉年二月

26

初一　周日

茂名路毛泽东旧居

Former Residence of Chairman Mao on Maoming Road

静安区茂名北路 120 弄 5-9 号
5-9 Lane 120, North Maoming Road, Jing'an District

1924 年 2 月底毛泽东来上海时住所

1924 年第一次国共合作达成后，毛泽东在国民党一大当选中央候补执行委员，在国民党中央上海执行部工作时的寓所，是一幢两楼两底的石库门房子。市级文物保护单位。

It is the residence where Mao Zedong lived when he was elected as the candidate executive member of CPC Central Committee at the First National Congress of KMT and worked in Shanghai Office of KMT, after CPC and KMT agreed upon the first CPC-KMT cooperation in 1924. It is a two-story Shikumen house with two rooms on each floor. It is a heritage site under municipal protection.

FEB. 27. 2017 MONDAY

2017.2

农历丁酉年二月

27

初二　周一

龙抬头

华懋公寓（锦江宾馆北楼）

Cathay Mansion (North Building of Jinjiang Hotel)

黄浦区茂名南路 59 号
59 South Maoming Road, Huangpu District

1972 年 2 月 28 日《中美上海联合公报》在此发布

现上海锦江饭店北楼，以典型的哥特式建筑风格著称。自 1927 年建成，就是众多多军政要领、社会名流下榻之处。1972 年《中美上海公报》在此发布。市级文物保护单位。

As the predecessor of Jin Jiang Hotel – the first state guesthouse in Shanghai, the Cathay Mansion was built in 1927, and has received many military essentials, intellectuals, renowned actors and actresses, business magnates and other celebrities. It is now a historical and cultural site protected at the municipal level.

28

初三　周二

影像·中国
上海地标
2017

叁
March
月

太原别墅

Taiyuan Villa

徐汇区太原路 160 号
160 Taiyuan Road, Xuhui District

上世纪 20 年代建成，仿照法国路易十四皇宫设计建造，被誉为上海法式建筑的经典之作。又称马歇尔公馆，1945 年至 1947 年初，乔治·马歇尔曾下榻此处调解国共两党和谈。

Designed and built following the royal palace of King Louis XIV, it was completed in the 1920s and honored as a classical work of French architecture in Shanghai. George Marshall once stayed here from 1945 to early 1947 to mediate the peace talks between Kuomintang and the Communist Party of China. Hence it is also called the Marshall Mansion.

MAR. 1. 2017 WEDNESDAY　2017.3　农历丁酉年二月

1

初四　周三

中国左翼作家联盟成立大会会址纪念馆

The League of the Left-Wing Writers Museum

虹口区多伦路 201 弄 2 号
2 Lane 201 Duolun Road, Hongkou District

1930 年 3 月 2 日“左联”成立

1930 年中国左翼作家联盟召开成立大会的建筑，现辟为革命历史纪念馆，共展出实物、文献和照片 400 多件，1990 年向公众开放。市级文物保护单位。

Composed of two garden villas of three-storied drywall and brick-wood structure, the museum houses more than 2,000 pieces of artifacts, materials and books, and is mainly dedicated to the publicity and the research of, the collection and custody of materials related to the League of Left-Wing Writers. It is a municipality protected historic and cultural site.

2

初五　周四

上海展览中心
Shanghai Exhibiting Center(SEC)

静安区延安中路 1000 号
1000 Middle Yan'an Rd., JingAn District

1955 年 3 月建成

建国后上海最早的会展场所，原名“中苏友好大厦”，上海地标之一，俄罗斯古典主义建筑风格。举行过许多重大政治、外事活动，全市主要的会议和展览场馆，对外交流窗口。

It is a pioneering exhibition site ever established after the founding of P.R.C. , primitively named “The Sino Soviet Friendship Mansion” and one of the significant landmarks of the city, profiled as the classical Russian style architecture. As the city's major meeting & exhibiting venue and external communication window, many political events and foreign affairs activities were held and witnessed hereon.

3

初六　周五

野生动物园

Wild Animal Park

浦东新区南六公路 178 号

178 Nanliu Highway, Pudong New Area

春秋两季是野生动物园最佳旅游时节

集野生动物饲养、展览、繁育保护、科普教育与休闲娱乐为一体。在这儿既能零距离认知大自然野趣，又可感受人与动物之间的和谐。国家 5A 景区。

The park integrates the functions of wild animal raising, exhibiting, breeding, protecting, and science popularization, recreation and entertainment. It provides close interactions with the nature and its rustic charm as well as a taste of the harmony between mankind and animals. It is a 5A-rated national tourist attraction.

4

初七　周六

蔡元培故居

Former Residence of CaiYuanpei

静安区华山路 303 弄 16 号

16 Lane 303, Huashan Road, Jing'an District

现代著名革命家、教育家、政治家蔡元培先生在上海生活工作和从事革命活动的居所，为一幢三层英式花园洋房，是国内保存最完好的一处蔡元培故居。市级文物保护单位。

It is the residence where Mr. CaiYuanpei, the famous revolutionist, educator and politician in modern times, lived, worked and conducted revolutionary activities in Shanghai. It is a three-story British garden house and one of the best preserved residences of CaiYuanpei in China. It is a heritage site under municipal protection.

5

初八 周日

惊蛰

犹太难民纪念馆
Jewish Refugees Museum

虹口区长阳路 62 号
62 Changyang Road, Hongkou District

1933 年 3 月大批犹太人来沪避难；2007 年 3 月该馆开放

上海仅存的两座犹太会堂旧址之一，二战期间是在沪犹太难民们聚会和举行宗教仪式的场所。整个上海关于犹太难民历史和实物资料最为齐全的地方。

Located at the former site of one of the only two remaining Jewish Synagogues in Shanghai, it was a venue where Jewish refugees in Shanghai gathered and held religious rites during the World War II. The museum features the most complete history and material objects of Jewish refugees in Shanghai, and it is a place that Jews will never miss when they come to Shanghai.

6

初九 周一

真如寺
Zhenru Temple

普陀区真如镇兰溪路 399 号
399 Lanxi Road, Zhenru Town, Putuo District

原名“万寿寺”，俗称“大庙”，上海著名佛寺，全国文物保护单位。大殿内现存梁、柱、枋斗拱等主体结构皆为元代原物，极为罕见。寺内七百年古银杏树至今枝繁叶茂。

The temple, formerly known as “temple of longevity (Wanshou-si)” and commonly known as “Damiao”, is a famous Buddhist temple in Shanghai and a cultural heritage under national protection. The existing beams, columns, brackets and other main structures in the main temple hall are extremely rare because they were all made in Yuan Dynasty. There is a 700-year -old ginkgo tree in the temple.

MAR. 7. 2017 TUESDAY　　2017.3　　农历丁酉年二月

7

初十　周二

平民女校旧址

Former Site of Commoner (Pingmin) Girls' School

静安区成都北路 7 弄 42 号 -44 号
42-44 Lane 7, North Chengdu Road, Jing'an District

1922 年中国共产党创办的第一所培养妇女干部的学校。师生中有陈望道、邵力子、李达、丁玲等名人。曾为中共二大会址。市级文物保护单位、上海妇女教育基地。

It is the first school founded by the CPC in 1922 to cultivate woman cadres. Among its graduates and faculties, there are celebrities such as Chen Wangdao, Shao Lizi, Li Da and Ding Ling. It was the site of the 2nd National Congress of the CPC. It is a heritage site under municipal protection and the base of women education in Shanghai.

十一　周三

妇女节

黄浦江水文化博物园

Huangpu River Museum of Water Culture

闵行区江川路 3805 号

3805 Jiangchuang Road, Minhang District

3 月 9 日“中国保护母亲河日”

一个多功能生态休闲园区，园区以黄浦江的历史、文化为内涵，以古朴、自然、野趣为格调，以科普教育、生态示范、黄浦江水系文献文物展示为主要功能。

A multifunctional ecological leisure park features the historical and cultural connotations of Huangpu River, the style of primitive simplicity, naturalness, and rustic charm, and the main function of science popularization education, ecological demonstration, the exhibition of literatures and cultural relics of the Huangpu River system.

9

十二　周四

申隆生态园

Shenlong Biopark

奉贤区青村镇申隆一村（原朱蒋村）

No.1 Shenlong Village, Qingcun Town, Fengxian District (former Zhujiang Village)

江南水乡特征的综合性绿色生态森林公园，集度假休闲、休养康复、观光会务为一体，有“南上海绿舟”之称。园中70%为生态林，25%为人工湖泊和河道，5%为林中道路。

As a comprehensive green ecological forest park with the characteristics of water towns in the South Yangtze River, it integrates the functions of vacation, rehabilitation, sightseeing and business together, and is known as "Oasis of South Shanghai". The park consists of 70% of ecological forest, 25% of artificial lakes and river channels, and 5% of routes in the forest.

10

十三　周五

共青国家森林公园

Gongqing National Forest Park

杨浦区军工路 2000 号
2000 Jungong Road, Yangpu District

植树节期间举行亲子雪松林认养活动

以森林为主要景观的特色公园，全园总占地 1965 亩，共种植 200 余种、30 多万株树木。分南北两园，北园着重森林景色，南园则小桥流水。南北园风格顾盼生姿。国家 4A 景区。

The park's identity is presented by its forest scenery. It covers an area of 1,965 mus and has more than 300,000 trees of over 200 species. The park consists of a north garden, which features the forest landscape, and a south garden with brooks and small bridges. The two gardens supplement each other, producing a special charm. It is a 4A-rated national tourist attraction.

MAR. 11. 2017 SATURDAY

2017.3

农历丁酉年二月

11

十四　周六

孙中山故居纪念馆

Museum of Sun Yat-Sen's Former Residence

黄浦区香山路 7 号
No.7 Xiangshan Road, Huangpu District

3 月 12 日孙中山先生逝世

由孙中山故居和孙中山文物馆组成，故居绝大部分是原物，文物馆展出孙中山先生生平事迹相关文物、手迹、资料三百余件。全国重点文物保护单位。

It consists of the former residence of Sun Yat-Sen and the Sun Yat-Sen Museum; the former's most collections are the original articles of Mr. Sun Yat-Sen and the latter displays over three hundred pieces of relics, manuscripts, and materials related to Mr. Sun Yat-Sen. It is an important heritage site under state protection

MAR. 12. 2017 SUNDAY

2017.3

农历丁酉年二月

12

十五　周日

植树节

虹口足球场

Hongkou Football Stadium

虹口区东江湾路 444 号
444 East Jiangwan Road, Hongkou District

1999 年 3 月中旬启用

中国第一座专业足球场。中国足球超级联赛（原甲 A 联赛）上海申花足球俱乐部主场，还设有室内游泳池、乒乓房、桌球房、足球射门训练场等全方位的体育娱乐设施。

The Hongkou Football Stadium is the first professional football stadium in China, and also the home court of Chinese Football Association Super League (formerly C League) and Shanghai Greenland Shenhua F.C. The stadium also features the indoor swimming pool, Ping-Pong room, billiard room, shooting training ground and other sports and entertainment facilities.

MAR. 13. 2017 MONDAY

2017.3

农历丁酉年二月

13

十六　周一

公安博物馆

Police Museum

黄浦区瑞金南路 518 号
518 South Ruijin Road, Huangpu District

国内首座公安专题博物馆，是目前世界上规模较大的警察题材博物馆。设公安史馆、刑事侦查馆、警用装备馆、情景互动射击馆、英烈馆等十二个分馆。国家二级博物馆。

It is the first public-security-themed museum in China and a relatively large police-themed museum in the world. It is a Grade-Two national museum.

14

十七　周二

大宁灵石公园
Daning-Lingshi Park

静安区广中西路 288 号
288 West Guangzhong Road, Jing'an District

每年 3 月 29 日前有郁金香展，4 月有爱鸟周

占地 68 万平方米，浦西排位第二的大型生态景观型城市公园和集中绿地。上海市城市总体规划确定的三大绿地之一。上海市文明公园，上海十大魅力景点之一。园内有 19 米高的人造山。

Covering an area of 680,000m^2, Daning-Lingshi Park is the second largest ecological landscape urban park in Puxi, the largest concentrated green space, and also one of three green spaces under the Urban Master Planning of Shanghai. Moreover, it is one of Shanghai's civilization parks and one of Shanghai's Top 10 Charming Scenic Spots. The park features a 19-meter-tall man-made mountain.

15

十八　周三

国际消费者权益日

新场古镇

Xinchang Ancient Town

浦东新区新场镇
Xinchang Town, Pudong New Area

每年 3 月中旬 –4 月底，古镇的桃园内有桃花节

一座因盐而成、因盐而兴的 800 年江南古镇。保存有 15 万平方米的成片古建筑，1200 米元、明、清时代的石驳岸，以及 69 座古代仪门。入选“中国历史文化名镇”。

It is an ancient town built and prosperous for salt in southeast China, with a history of 800 years. With 150,000 square meters of ancient buildings, 1,200-meter stone revetment preserved from Yuan, Ming and Qing Dynasties and 69 ancient Yimen (doors of etiquette), it has been listed into the “Chinese Famous Cultural & Historic Towns”.

MAR. 16. 2017 THURSDAY

2017.3

农历丁酉年二月

16

十九　周四

张充仁纪念馆
Zhang Chongren Memorial

闵行区七宝镇蒲溪广场 75 号
75 Puxi Square, Qibao Town, Minhang District

2003 年 3 月 17 日开馆

展示一代雕塑大师张充仁先生的生平事迹和艺术成就的博物馆。是一座明清风格木结构江南庭院。有序厅、饮誉欧洲、画室春秋、雕塑泰斗四大展区。国家三级博物馆。

This Grade-Three national museum shows the life story and artistic achievements of Mr. Zhang Chongren, a great respected master of sculpture.

MAR. 17. 2017 FRIDAY

2017.3

农历丁酉年二月

17

二十　周五

虹桥国际机场
Hongqiao International Airport

长宁区虹桥路 2550 号
2550 Hongqiao Road, Changning District

1921 年 3 月定名虹桥机场

始建于 1907 年，前身是民国虹桥机场，建国后一度为军用机场。上世纪 60 年代经国家批准改扩建为民用机场，与浦东国际机场形成“一市两场”的上海空港运行新格局。

Built in 1907, the predecessor of it was the Hongqiao Airport during the Republic of China, and once served as a military airport after 1949. In the 1960s, it was rebuilt into a civil airport upon the approval of the state. It is now one of Shanghai's two international airports.

18

廿一 周六

三山会馆

Sanshan Guild Hall

黄浦区中山南路 1551 号
1551 South Zhongshan Road, Huangpu District

1927 年 3 月下旬上海工人第三次武装起义

建于清末宣统元年（1909），是上海唯一保存完好的晚清会馆建筑，也是唯一保存完好的上海工人三次武装起义遗址。市级文物保护单位。

Built in the first year in the reign of Emperor Xuantong in Qing Dynasty (1909), Sanshan Guild Hall is the only well preserved guild hall built in the late Qing Dynasty with high value of art appreciation. As the only historical site of the third armed uprisings launched by Shanghai workers, the building is now a municipality protected historic and cultural site.

19

廿二 周日

宋教仁墓
Song Jiaoren's Tomb

静安区共和新路 1555 号闸北公园内
inside Zhabei Park, 1555 Gonghexin Road, Jing'an District

1913 年 3 月宋教仁遇刺

近现代民主革命先行者、中国国民党和中华民国的主要缔造者之一、1913 年被袁世凯刺杀的宋教仁先生的墓葬，1924 年建成，原名宋公园。市级文物保护单位。

Completed in 1924, it is the tomb of Mr. Song Jiaoren, a pioneer of democratic revolution in themodern times, one of the key founders of KMT and Republic of China and who was assassinated by Yuan Shikai in 1913. Formerly known as Song's Park, it is a heritage site under municipal protection.

20

廿三　周一

春分

佘山国家森林公园

Sheshan National Forest Park

松江区佘山镇外青松公路 9258 号
9258 Outer Qingsong Highway, Sheshan Town, Songjiang District

3 月 21 日国家森林日

上海境内唯一的自然山林胜地，以人文荟萃的历史文化和宗教胜迹名闻遐迩，有护珠塔、秀道者塔、天主教堂、天文台等国家、市级文物保护单位。国家 4A 景区。

It's the only natural mountainous forest site in Shanghai and is known for its historical, cultural and religious attractions, such as Huzhu Pogoda, Xiudaozhe Pogoda, Catholic Church, observatory and other historical and cultural sites protected at national or municipal level. It is a 4A-rated national tourist attraction.

21

廿四　周二

杨树浦水厂

Yangshupu Water Plant

杨浦区杨树浦路 830 号
830 Yangshupu Road, Yangpu District

建于清末的中国供水行业建厂最早、生产能力最大的全国第一座现代化水厂。水厂城堡式厂房被命名为“上海市优秀历史建筑”。全国重点文物保护单位。

Built in the late Qing Dynasty, it was the earliest modern water plant with the largest production capacity in China. The castle-like buildings of the plant were honored as the “outstanding historical buildings in Shanghai”. It is an important heritage site under state protection.

22

廿五　周三

世界水日

东平国家森林公园

Dongping National Forest Park

崇明区东平林场北沿公路 2188 号
2188 Beiyan Highway, Dongping Forestry Farm, Chongming District

总面积 358 公顷，华东地区最大的平原人造森林，也是上海规模最大的森林公园。公园内动植物资源丰富，有野生植物近千种，野生动物几十种，候鸟将近 160 种。国家 4A 景区。

With a total area of 358 hectares, it is the largest man-made forest in Eastern China and also the biggest forest park in Shanghai. It has rich and diverse animal and plant resources, including nearly 1,000 species of wild plants, several dozen wild animals, and nearly 160 species of migrant birds. It is a 4A-rated national tourist attraction.

23

廿六 周四

顾村公园

Gucun Park

宝山区沪太路 4788 号
4788 Hutai Road, Gucun Town, Baoshan District

每年 3 月中下旬至 4 月中下旬樱花节

上海市最大的郊野公园，集生态防护、景观观赏、休闲健身、文化娱乐、旅游度假等功能于一体。公园植被丰富，尤其是春季赏樱花深受游客欢迎。国家 4A 景区。

It is the largest suburban park in Shanghai and integrates many functions, such as ecological protection, landscaping, leisure and bodybuilding, culture and entertainment, tourism and vacation. Rich vegetation in the park, especially sakura flowers in full blossom in spring, wins the favor of visitors. It is a 4A-rated national tourist attraction.

24

廿七　周五

广场公园

Square Park

延安东路至延安中路（西藏南路至茂名南路）
Along with East Yan'an Road and Middle Yan'an Road (from South Xizang Road to South Maoming Road)

也称延中绿地，是延安中路上的大型公共绿地，位于静安、卢湾、黄浦三区交界处，是集观赏游览、休闲娱乐于一体的开放式都市花园，免费开放。上海市五星级公园。

Square Park is also known as Yanzhong Green Space, a free open city garden integrating the functions of sightseeing, leisure and entertainment. It is a five-star park in Shanghai.

MAR. 25. 2017 SATURDAY　2017.3　农历丁酉年二月

25

廿八　周六

南京大戏院（上海音乐厅）

Nanjing Grand Theatre (Shanghai Concert Hall)

黄浦区延安东路 523 号
523 East Yan'an Road, Huangpu District

1930 年 3 月 26 日开业

1930 年建成开业。1959 年更名为上海音乐厅。欧洲传统建筑风格，观众厅大跨度的穹顶还原真实音色，成为国内早期音乐厅建筑的经典之作。市级文物保护单位。

Built and opened in 1930 and then renamed as Nanjing Grand Theatre after 1949, Shanghai Concert Hall got its name in 1959, which is used till now. It is a heritage site under municipal protection.

MAR. 26. 2017 SUNDAY

2017.3

农历丁酉年二月

26

廿九　周日

基督教慕尔堂（沐恩堂）

Moore Memorial Church (Immanuel Lutheran Church)

黄浦区西藏中路 316 号
316 Middle Xizang Road, Huangpu District

由美国基督教监理公会传教士李德创立，建有高大钟楼，是当时远东著名教堂。外观为美国学院复兴哥特式。1958 年改名“沐恩堂”。市级文物保护单位。

Founded by C.F.Reid, a Christian missionary of American Association of Christian Supervision, Moore Memorial Church, with a tall bell tower, was a famous church in Shanghai and even the Far East then. It was renamed “Immanuel Lutheran Church” in 1958. It is a heritage site under municipal protection.

27

三十　周一

泰晤士小镇

Thames Town

松江区三新北路 900 弄
Lane 900, North Sanxin Road, Songjiang District

3 月—5 月游玩最佳季

总占地面积约一平方公里，从整体布局到一砖一瓦都体现了原汁原味的欧洲风情。是一个具有居住、旅游、休闲等多项功能的大型社区。

The town, with a total area of about one square kilometer, is a large community featuring dwelling, travel, relaxation and other functions, and displaying the European style of original taste and flavor through its overall layout and every single brick and tile.

28

初一　周二

徐志摩旧居

The Former residence of Xu Zhimo

静安区延安中路 913 弄
Lane 913, Middle Yan'an Road, Jing'an District

1929 年 3 月 29 日泰戈尔到上海曾住此处

现代著名诗人、"新月派"的代表、散文家徐志摩在上海的故居。原址是一幢三层楼的新式里弄，老式石库门洋房。1929 年泰戈尔来访曾在此居住。

It is the former residence of Xu Zhimo, a modern famous poet, representative of "Crescent School" and proser, in Shanghai. The original residence was a three-story alley of new style, an old Shikumen foreign-style house. Rabindranath Tagore stayed here when he visited China in 1929.

29

初二　周三

龙华寺

Longhua Temple

徐汇区龙华路 2853 号

2853 Longhua Road, Xuhui District

每年农历三月初三龙华庙会

江南地区最古老的寺庙之一，始建于宋代。1953 年政府重修各殿佛像、殿宇，新建藏经楼等。市级文物保护单位。

Built in the Song Dynasty, Longhua Temple is one of the oldest temples in the Jiangnan region (southern part of the Yangtze River). In 1953 the Buddha statues and temple halls were restored and a new library of Buddhist scriptures was built by the government. The temple is a heritage site protected at the municipal level.

30

初三 周四

世纪公园
Century Park

浦东新区锦绣路 1001 号
1001 Jinxiu Road, Pudong New Area

3 月底最佳游玩季

上海最大的富有自然特征的生态型城市公园。占地 140.3 公顷，是繁华中的一片宁静、水泥森林中的一片“绿肺”。国家 4A 景区。

It is the largest ecological urban park with natural elements in Shanghai. Covering an area of 140.3 hectares, it provides a land of serenity against the din and bustle, and a “green lung” amid the concrete jungles. It is a 4A-rated national tourist attraction.

31

初四 周五

影像·中国
上海地标
2017

肆
April
月

静安公园

Jing'an Garden

静安区南京西路 1649 号
1649 West Nanjing Road, Jing'an District

4 月 1 日茶花展

上海闹市中心的公园。有林荫大道、中心广场、东草坪、西草坪、茶花园等五大著名园景。每年 2 ~ 5 月茶花相继开放，吸引无数游人驻足。上海市五星级公园。

As a park located at downtown center of Shanghai, Jing'an Garden boasts five famous landscapes, which are the boulevard, the central square, east lawn, west lawn, tea garden. It is a five-star park in Shanghai.

1

初五　周六

愚人节

宛平 88
No.88 Wanping Road

徐汇区宛平南路 88 号
No.88, South Wanping Road, Xuhui District

地处徐家汇商圈核心，由金座与银座两幢办公大厦，三幢高层精装住宅楼构成。拥有良好的商业、教育、医疗及绿化等配套设施。金座现为东方财富信息股份有限公司新的总部大厦。

Located at the core area of Xujiahui, the project consists of two office buildings(Gold and Silver Building)and three high-rise residential buildings with refined decoration. It sits on quality supporting facilities as commerce, education, medical care and greening and so on. Gold Building is the new HQ of East Money Information Co., Ltd..

2

初六　周日

邹容墓

Zou Rong's Tomb

徐汇区华泾路 1000 弄西
West of Lane 1000, Huajing Road, Xuhui District

邹容 1905 年 4 月 3 日死于上海狱中

近代著名民主革命烈士，以其著述《革命军》扬名的邹容之墓。墓区占地 1 亩余，坐北朝南。墓址有于右任撰文及丹书书碑。市级文物保护单位。

It is the tomb of Zou Rong who was a famous martyr of the democratic revolution in modern times and was known for his work *The Revolutionary Army*. The tomb covers an area of over 1 Chinese acre and faces the south. By the tomb, there is a stone tablet inscribed with writings of Yu Youren. It is a heritage site under municipal protection.

3

初七 周一

寒食节

福寿园

Fu Shou Yuan

青浦区外青松公路 7270 弄 600 号
600 Lane 7270, the outer Qingsong Road, Qingpu District

上海市一级公墓，占地一千多亩，地处青浦境内，毗邻松江，坐落在佘山、天马山和淀山湖之间，风水极佳，多位名人安息其中。

With the magnificent scenery, it is a first-class cemetery in Shanghai, covering an area of over 1,000 Chinese acres, located in Qingpu District, adjacent to Songjiang, situated between She-shan, Tianmashan and Dian Shan Lake. Many celebrities were buried here.

4

初八　周二

清明节

月湖雕塑公园

Sculpture Park

松江区佘山镇林荫新路 1158 号
1158 New Linyin Road, Sheshan Town, Songjiang District

集现代雕塑艺术、现代景观艺术、现代建筑艺术以及高档休闲于一体的综合性艺术园区，拥有上海面积最大的人工湖。园内有雕塑作品 80 余件。国家 4A 景区。

It is a comprehensive art park integrating modern sculpture art, modern landscape art, modern architectural art and high-end entertainment. It has the largest artificial lake in Shanghai and over 80 pieces of sculpture. It is a 4A-rated national tourist attraction.

5

初九　周三

闵行体育公园

Minhang Sports Park

闵行区新镇路 456 号
456 Xinzhen Road, Minhang District

3-4 月郁金香展，7-8 月荷花睡莲展

上海市首座以体育命名的大型城市主题公园，免费开放。设计和建设以自然景观为主，设有体育场馆区、热带风暴水上乐园、湿地生态园等 10 个景区。上海市五星级公园。

It is Shanghai's first sports named park and first large city theme park, free to the public. It is a five-star park in Shanghai.

6

初十　周四

鲜花港

Flower Port

浦东新区东海农场振东路 2 号
2 Zhendong Road, Donghai Farm, Pudong New Area

以花农培训、花卉种植、新品展示、新品研发、种苗出口为主的现代农业示范园区。在此可春赏郁金香、夏赏荷、秋赏菊。国家 4A 景区。

It is a modern agricultural demonstration park that focuses on flower farmer trainings, flower planting, new species exhibition, new product development, and seedlings export. At the port, you may enjoy tulips in spring, lotus flowers in summer and chrysanthemums in fall. It is a 4A-rated national tourist attraction.

APR. 7. 2017 FRIDAY

2017.4

农历丁酉年三月

7

十一　周五

上海交通大学
Shanghai Jiao Tong University

徐汇区华山路 1954 号
1954 Huashan Road, Xuhui District

4 月 8 日校庆日

前身为 1896 年创立的南洋公学，1921 年改组为交通大学。具理工特色，涵盖理、工、医、经、管、文、法等 9 大学科的综合性研究型大学，知名校友有蔡元培、邹韬奋、钱学森等。

As one of the first batch of national key universities designated as Project 211 and Project 985 institutions, Shanghai Jiao Tong University, featured by science and engineering, is a comprehensive research-oriented university with 9 departments of Science, Engineering, Medicine, Economics, Management, Literature, Law, etc.

8

十二　周六

江湾体育场（上海市体育场）
Jiangwan Sports Center (Shanghai Stadium)

杨浦区国和路 346 号
346 Guohe Road, Yangpu District

1933 年起由旧上海市政府直接主持筹建的体育场，是国民党“江湾大上海计划”的遗产，曾有“远东第一体育场”之称，著名建筑设计师董大酉的作品。市级文物保护单位。

As a stadium built in 1933 under the direct organization of the then Shanghai municipal government, the ever called the “First Stadium in the Far East” is still in the use now. It is a historical and cultural site protected at the municipal level.

APR. 9. 2017 SUNDAY

2017.4

农历丁酉年三月

9

十三　周日

陈云故居暨青浦革命历史纪念馆

Former Residence of Chen Yun and Qingpu Revolutionary History Memorial

青浦区练塘镇朱枫公路 3516 号
3516 Zhufeng Highway, Liantang Town, Qingpu District

展示陈云同志生平业绩的纪念馆，用建筑语言、馆藏革命文物、陈云铜像等表现崇高的纪念主题，又与周边民宅融为一体，体现了江南水乡独具的韵味。国家 4A 景区。

It displays the achievements of Mr. Chen Yun during his lifetime. The lofty memorial theme is represented by architectural language, the revolutionary relics in its collection, and the cooper statue of Chen Yun. The structure makes a perfect blend with the surrounding folk residences, striking a note unique to the water towns in south China. It is a 4A-rated national tourist attraction.

10

十四　周一

嘉定孔庙
Jiangding Confucius Temple

嘉定区嘉定镇南大街 183 号
183 South Street, Jiading Town, Jiading District

公元前 479 年 4 月 11 日孔子逝世

又名学宫，始建于南宋嘉定年间，有吴中第一之称，是目前国内比较完整的孔庙之一。建国后两次大修，现辟有中国科举博物馆。全国重点文物保护单位。

Also known as the Study Palace, it was first built during the Jiangding period of the South Song Dynasty, once reputed as the No.1 temple in Jiangsu Province, and is currently among the relatively well-preserved Confucius Temples in China. After the People's Republic of China was established, it has gone through two major renovations and now has in it the Imperial Examination Museum of China. It is an important heritage site under national protection.

11

十五　周二

紫藤园

Wisteria Garden

嘉定区博乐路 45 号
45 Bole Road, Jiading District

4 月进入紫藤花期，月底花期结束

1997 年 9 月，为纪念嘉定区与日本冈山县和气町友好交往而建，布局兼有中国山水园林和部分日本造园风格。园内有优良紫藤 100 余株，每年 4 月，紫花串串，芳香诱人。

Built to commemorate the friendly exchanges between Jiading District and Wake, Okayama Prefecture, Japan, the garden has an overall layout with characters of Chinese landscape gardens and some Japanese gardening styles. There are over 100 strains of wisteria of good variety which blossom and emit attracting aroma every April.

APR. 12. 2017 WEDNESDAY

2017.4

农历丁酉年三月

12

十六　周三

古藤园

Ancient Wisteria Garden

闵行区临沧路 148 号
148 Lincang Road, Minhang District

4 月中旬紫藤花最美季

因有明代嘉靖年间诗人董宜阳手植的古紫藤而得园名，园为保护这株沪上最古老的紫藤而建。园内四季如春，景色怡人。

Named after the ancient wisteria planted by the poet Dong Yiyang during the years of Jiajing in Ming Dynasty, the garden was built for the protection of the strain of this oldest wisteria in Shanghai. There is spring-like weather all the year around and pleasant scenery.

13

十七 周四

太阳岛国际俱乐部

Sun Island International Club

青浦区沈太路 2588 号
2588 Shentai Road, Qingpu District

3—5 月最佳观光季

集山水、园林和遗迹为一体，是个风景悠然而富有情趣的度假胜地。中国五大古灯塔之一“泖塔”（全国重点文物保护单位）已有 1200 年历史。国家 4A 景区。

Being a scenic and tasteful choice for holiday-makers, it is an integration of the elements of mountains, rivers, gardens and historical relics. “Mao Beacon”, one of the five major ancient beacons in China and a historical and cultural site protected at the national level, has a history of 1,200 years. The club is a 4A-rated national tourist attraction.

APR. 14. 2017 FRIDAY

2017.4

农历丁酉年三月

14

十八　周五

练塘老街

Liantang Old Street

青浦区练塘镇
Liantang Town, Qingpu District

千年老街，得名传说一为三国东吴在此修建操练水军的池塘，二为五代时高州刺史章仔钧及练夫人曾居住。茭白节、江浙沪特色小吃、苏州刺绣、糖画、捏面人著名。

There are two legends for naming of this one-thousand-year old street: one is that here there was a pond built by Eastern Wu of the Three Kingdoms for practicing the navy, and the other is that Gaozhou prefectural governor Zhang Zijun and his wife Lian Jun once lived here during the Five Dynasties Period. The key tour experience in this old street includes Wild Rice Shoots Festival, local flavors of Jiangsu, Zhejiang and Shanghai, Suzhou embroidery, Sugar Painting and Dough Figurine.

APR. 15. 2017 SATURDAY

2017.4

农历丁酉年三月

15

十九　周六

玻璃博物馆

Museum of Glass

宝山区长江西路 685 号
685 West Changjiang Road, Baoshan District

2015 年 4 月 16 日成为国家 4A 级旅游景区

曾是玻璃工厂厂区，现为非盈利私立博物馆。向参观者传达玻璃的无限可能，创造了全新的参观体验。该馆和所在 G+ 玻璃主题园已成为国家 4A 景点。

The Shanghai Museum of Glass (formerly a glass factory) is now a non-profit private museum under the administration of Shanghai Municipal Administration Commission of Cultural Heritage. It delivers the infinite possibility of glass to visitors and creates a brand-new visitor experience. This museum and the G+ Glass Theme Park have become national 4A -rated scenic spots.

16

二十　周日

复活节

传媒文化园
Shanghai Media and Cultural Park

静安区昌平路 1000 号
1000 Changping Road, Jing'an District

2005 年 4 月成为上海首批 18 个创意产业集聚区之一

前身是上海窗钩厂，现为以影视制作、网络图片、艺术摄影、工业和建筑创意设计等为特色的创意园区，有以网络图片设计为主导和以建筑、工业创意设计为主导的两大特色产业。

Formerly known as the Shanghai Window Hook Factory, it is a creative park that features film & television production, internet pictures, art photography, industrial and building creative design, with two leading characteristic industries of internet pictures design and building as well as industrial creative design.

APR. 17. 2017 MONDAY

2017.4

农历丁酉年三月

17

廿一　周一

世博源

The River Mall

浦东新区世博大道 1368 号
1368 Expo Avenue, Pudong New Area

2014 年 4 月开业

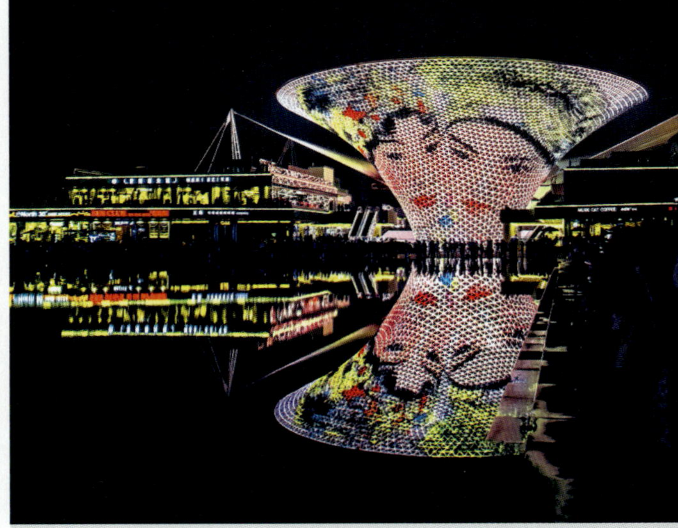

由世博轴改建的超广域型综合购物中心，空间设计贯穿“水”元素，以江河流水为主题，形成二街五区的布局，充满了自然元素和艺术气息。

It is a super-large shopping complex rebuilt from Expo Axis. With the element “water” running through the space design and the theme of flowing rivers, it features a layout of two streets and five districts, full of natural elements and artistic atmosphere.

18

廿二　周二

热带风暴
the Tropical Storm Theme Park

闵行区新镇路 78 号
78 Xinzhen Road, Minhang District

夏季最为适宜

目前亚洲最大的露天水上乐园之一，占地 130 亩。有 30 多种精彩刺激的水上游乐项目，其中“霹雳河”是目前亚洲最长的水上乐园内河，“风暴滩”是亚洲最大的人工海浪池。

It is one of the largest Asian opern-air waterpark covering an area of 134 Chinese acres, among which the PILI River ranks the longest inland river of the Asia's theme park,and the STORM Sandbeach the biggest artificial sea wave tank as well. More than thirty kinds of thrilling surfacing entertainment projects and services are provided here.

19

廿三 周三

陕西北路
North Shaanxi Road

上海市静安区境内
Jing'an District, Shanghai

上海著名的文化休闲街，租界时期名为“西摩路”，沿街有荣宗敬故居、西摩会堂、民国宋氏家族旧居、犹太住宅等21处名人故居和优秀历史建筑。中国历史文化名街。

It is a famous street of leisure and culture in Shanghai and was called “Seymour Road” in the foreign settlement period. Along the street are 21 former residences of famous persons and historic architectures, including the former residence of Rong Zongjing, the Ohel Rachel Synagogue, the former residence of the Song Family in the Republic of China, and a Jewish residence. It is a famous historical and cultural street in China.

APR. 20. 2017 THURSDAY

2017.4

农历丁酉年三月

20

廿四　周四

谷雨

崇明新城公园

New City Park in Chongming

崇明区崇明大道（近江帆路）
Chongming Street (close to Jiangfan Road), Chongming District

位于生态岛崇明的开放式公园，按功能分为庆典广场、缓冲林带、公园博物馆等十大区域。地形高低起伏、水体及岸线曲折回转，植物群落丰富多变。

It is located in the eco-friendly Chongming Island with an open setup, divided into ten areas according to their functions, including Ceremony Square, Cushion Forest, and Park Museum. The park features rolling grounds, winding waters and shorelines, as well as diversified vegetation.

21

廿五 周五

华东政法大学

East China University of Political Science and Law

长宁区万航渡路 1575 号
1575 Wanhangdu Road, Changning District

4 月 22 日世界法律日

1952 年创办的新中国第一批高等政法院校之一，2007 年更名。前身为圣约翰大学。现为以法学学科为主，兼有经济学、管理学等学科的市属重点大学，有长宁、松江两个校区。

Amongst the first batch of higher educational institutions of political science and law established in the People's Republic of China, it is a leading university under the administration of Shanghai municipal government, offering programs in Economics, Management, Literature, Science, etc. with the discipline of law playing a dominant role. In March 2007, it was renamed as "East China University of Political Science and Law" upon the approval of the Ministry of Education.

22

廿六 周六

世界法律日

嘉定区图书馆
Central Library of Jiading Library

嘉定区裕民南路 1288 号
1288 South Yumin Road, Jiading District

4 月 23 日世界读书日

该馆建筑沿袭江南书院风格，屋顶形似打开的书籍，将古朴风韵与现代气质完美融合，被美国《Interior Design》杂志评为“世界最美公共图书馆”之一。

The library follows the style of academies of classic learning in the regions south of Yangtze River. The roof like an opened book creates the perfect integration of plain charm and modern look. It is rated by the American magazine *Interior Design* as one of “the World’s Most Beautiful Public Library”.

APR. 23. 2017 SUNDAY

2017.4

农历丁酉年三月

23

廿七　周日

滨江森林公园

Riverside Forest Park

浦东新区高桥镇凌桥高沙滩 3 号
3 Lingqiaogao Beach, Gaoqiao Town, Pudong New Area

每年 4 月中旬杜鹃展

上海森林覆盖率最高的郊野森林公园，地处黄浦江、长江、东海“三水并流”之处，是从水路进入上海的门户景观。规划面积 300 公顷，是上海“绿肺”。上海市五星级公园。

It is a suburb forest park with the highest forest coverage in Shanghai and also the gateway landscape of waterway to Shanghai. It is a five-star park in Shanghai.

24

廿八　周一

徐家汇公园
Xujiahui Park

徐汇区肇嘉浜路 889 号
889 Zhaojiabang Road, Xuhui District

每年 4 月初绿地音乐节

沪上第一家音乐主题公园，免费开放，内有三大名胜：纪念烟囱、公园湖和观景桥。其中观景桥犹如穿越时光隧道，感受上海今昔变迁。上海市五星级公园。

The park has three attractions: the Memorial Chimney, the Park Lake and the Scenic Overlooks Bridge, a bridge that like a time tunnel showing people the yesterday, today and tomorrow appearance of Shanghai. It is a five-star park in Shanghai.

25

廿九　周二

银行博物馆
Bank Museum

浦东新区浦东大道 9 号世纪金融大厦 7 楼
7th Floor, Century Finance Tower, 9 Pudong Avenue, Pudong New Area

2000 年 4 月开馆

上海乃至全国首家金融行业博物馆，以上海近代银行发展史为主线，通过翔实的史料实物及丰富生动的展示手段，浓缩了上海 150 年的银行沧桑。国家三级博物馆。

As a Grade-Three national museum, Shanghai Bank Museum is the first museum of financial industry in Shanghai and even the country, which concentrates the vicissitudes of the banks in Shanghai over 150 years.

APR. 26. 2017 WEDNESDAY 2017.4 农历丁酉年四月

26

初一 周三

滴水湖

Dishui Lake

浦东新区临港新城环湖西一路
No.1 West Huanhu Road, Lingang New City, Pudong New Area

又名芦潮湖，是填海造陆开挖的人工湖，总面积5.56平方公里，是浦东南汇新城的中心湖泊，现为国家水利风景区。环湖地带是南汇新城城市综合功能服务区。

Also called the Luchao Lake, it is an artificial lake excavated for sea reclamation, covering a total area of 5.56 square kilometers. As a central lake in Nanhui New City, Pudong, it is now a national water conservancy scenic spot. The area around the lake is the comprehensive functional service area of Nanhui New City.

27

初二　周四

梅赛德斯 – 奔驰文化中心

Mercedes-Benz Arena

浦东新区世博大道 1200 号
1200 Expo Avenue, Pudong New Area

2010 年世博会前夕运营

上海世博会最重要的永久性场馆。整体造型呈飞碟状，不同角度不同时间呈现出不同形态。世界一流水准的综合演艺、艺术展示、时尚娱乐集聚区。上海旅游和文化娱乐新地标。

Mercedes-Benz Arena is one of the most important permanent venues of Shanghai World Expo. The overall design shaped like a flying disc presents different shapes from different angles and in different spaces. In the future, it will become an area of world class gathering comprehensive performing arts, art display, fashion and entertainment, as well as a new landmark of Shanghai tourism.

APR. 28. 2017 FRIDAY

2017.4

农历丁酉年四月

28

初三　周五

金山农民画生态休闲园
Ecological Leisure Park of Jinshan Peasant Painting

金山区枫泾镇北部中洪村
Zhonghong Village, North Fengjing Town, Jinshan District

2008 年 4 月 29 日正式命名“中国农民画村”

位于金山区枫泾镇中洪村，文化底蕴丰厚，将本土民居与当地地形地貌有机结合在一起，融旅游、作画、购画、观光、休闲、餐饮于一体。

Located at the Zhonghong Village of Fengjing Town in Jinshan District, it has rich cultural deposits and distinctive features, which combines local dwellings with local landforms and integrates travel, painting, painting-buying, sightseeing, leisure and catering.

APR. 29. 2017 SATURDAY

2017.4

农历丁酉年四月

29

初四　周六

申报馆

Shun Pao Office Building

黄浦区汉口路 309 号
309 Hankou Road, Huangpu District

1872 年 4 月 30 日申报创刊

近代中国发行时间最久，被誉为研究中国近现代史“百科全书”的报纸——创办于 1872 年的《申报》编辑部所在地。一座 5 层钢筋混凝土结构的新古典主义的近代建筑。

The Shun Pao Office Building is the home of the editorial office of Shun Pao, a newspaper established in 1872. Being honored as the "encyclopedia" of the modern and contemporary Chinese history, Shun Pao boasts the longest time of publication. It is a five-floor early modern architecture.

30

初五　周日

影像·中国
上海地标
2017

伍
May
月
南浦大桥
NANPU BRIDGE
杨高南路
YANGGAO RD(S)
世纪大道
CENTURY AVE
陆家嘴金融贸易区
Lujiazui Financial Trade Zone

工人文化宫
Worker's Cultural Palace

黄浦区西藏中路 120 号
120 Middle Xizang Road, Huangpu District

1950 年成立。七层的主体建筑始建于 1929 年，古典欧罗巴建筑风采犹存。上海市优秀建筑保护单位。

Shanghai Worker's Cultural Palace was founded in 1950 and served as a venue for labors' to study culture, science and art and recreation in their spare time. The seven-storey main building was founded in 1929, and still maintains the classical Europa architectural style. It is an excellent building protection unit of Shanghai.

1

初六 周一

劳动节

澹园

Danyuan Garden

崇明区北门路与东门路交汇处
The intersection of Beimen Road and Dongmen Road of Chongming District

1987 年 5 月开放

崇明唯一仿古园林，有宝岛明珠微型公园之称。既有传统的花居形式，又有古色古香的苏州园林佳景，植有腊梅、香橼、石楠、胡颓子、拘骨、天竺、石笋等 70 多种古树名花。

It is the only antique garden in Chongming which is reputed as "Miniature Park and a Pearl on the Treasure Island". The garden not only maintains the traditional style of garden, but also has the antique scenery of Suzhou garden with more than 70 kinds of famed plants such as winter sweet, fructus citri, heather, elaeagnus pungens thunb, ilex cornuta, common nandina fruit and stalagmite.

2

初七 周二

话剧艺术中心
Dramatic Arts Centre

徐汇区安福路 288 号
288 Anfu Road, Xuhui District

5 月上海大学生话剧艺术节

国家级专业话剧团体、中国最优秀的话剧团体之一——上海话剧艺术中心的演出和办公场地。包含艺术剧院、戏剧沙龙、D6 空间等顶级、先锋演出和交流单元。

It is the site of performance and office of Shanghai Dramatic Arts Centre - one of national-level professional drama groups and China's most excellent drama groups. It consists of Arts Theatre, Drama Salon Studio D6 and other units for the top-grade, avant-garde performances and exchanges.

3

初八　周三

中国社会主义青年团中央机关旧址纪念馆

The Memorial Site of The Central Committee of the Socialist Youth League of China

黄浦区淮海中路 567 弄 6 号
6 Lane 567, Middle Huaihai Road, Huangpu District

1920 年 8 月中国共产主义青年团的前身——中国社会主义青年团在上海成立并设立中央机关的地方，为两层楼砖木结构石库门建筑。全国重点文物保护单位。

It is the place where the Socialist Youth League of China, the former of the Communist Youth League of China, was established and set up its central organ in Shanghai in August 1920. It is a two-story Shikumen building with a brick-and-wood structure and an important heritage site under state protection.

4

初九 周四

青年节

1920 年毛泽东寓所旧址
Former Residence of Mao Zedong in 1920

静安区安义路 63 号
63 Anyi Road, Jing'an District

1920 年 5 月 5 日毛泽东来沪下榻此处

1920 年毛泽东率领“湖南驱张请愿团”，领导湖南在沪学生驱逐湖南军阀张敬尧，以及会见陈独秀讨论马列主义的地方，是一座两层砖木结构海派民居。市级文物保护单位。

It is the place where Mao Zedong led “Hunan Expelling-Zhang Petition Group”, particularly Hunan students studying in Shanghai, in 1920 to expel the warlord Zhang Jingyao from Hunan Province and where he discussed Marxism-Leninism with Chen Duxiu. It is a two-story Haipai residence with a brick-wooden structure and a heritage site under municipal protection.

5

初十　周五

立夏

中华职业教育社旧址

Site of Former National Association of Vocational Education of China

黄浦区雁荡路 80 号
80 Yandang Road, Huangpu District

1917 年 5 月 6 日创立

旧址是由黄炎培联络教育界、实业界知名人士发起、成立的中国第一个全国性教育团体——中华职业教育社的原址所在地，位于步行休闲街雁荡路。市级文物保护单位。

As a historical and cultural site protected at the municipal level, it is the location of the original address of the first national educational body in China - the National Association of Vocational Education of China cofounded by Huang Yanpei and celebrities in both education and business circles.

6

十一　周六

李白烈士故居

Former Residence of Martyr Li Bai

虹口区黄渡路 107 弄 15 号
15 Lane 107 Huangdu Road, Hongkou District

1948 年 5 月 7 日李白就义

长期从事中共地下电台工作、电影《永不消逝的电波》中“李侠”的原型、革命烈士李白的居所，三层砖木结构老式洋房，按已故裘慧英夫人回忆陈设。市级文物保护单位。

It is the former residence of the revolutionary martyr Li Bai who is the archetypal character of “Li Xia” in the film The Eternal Wave and who had engaged in the CPC underground radio work for a long term. It is an old three-story house with a brick-wooden structure and furnished with displays as memorized by the late Ms. Qiu Huiying. It is a heritage site under municipal protection.

7

十二 周日

吉云禅寺塔（青龙塔）

Pagoda of Jiyun Temple (Qinglong Pagoda)

青浦区白鹤镇青龙村

Qinglong Village, Baihe Town, Qingpu District

1979 年 5 月 8 日经修葺重新开放

上海最古老的塔。建于唐朝长庆年间，又名青龙塔，唐宋时巨港青龙镇遗存的本地稀有的实物古迹，是研究上海古代史、古建筑和佛教史的活化石。市级文物保护单位。

It is the oldest pagoda in Shanghai. Built during the Changqing period of the Tang Dynasty, it is a rare physical relic of Tang and Song Dynasties. It is a living fossil for the research of the ancient history, ancient architecture and the Buddhist history of Shanghai. It is a heritage site under municipal protection.

8

十三　周一

上海国际高尔夫球乡村俱乐部
Shanghai Golf & Country Club

青浦区朱家角镇盈朱路 961 号
961 Yingzhu Road, Zhujiajiao Town, Qingpu District

1991 年 5 月开放

坐落在风景秀丽的淀山湖畔，占地 103 万平方米，是国际标准的 18 洞高尔夫球场，有“上海威尼斯球场”之称，由世界著名的高尔夫球场设计大师罗伯特·琼斯二世设计。

Located beside the beautiful Dian Shan Lake and covering an area of 1,030,000 square meters, it is an 18-hole golf course of international standard, known as the “Venice stadium of Shanghai”. It was designed by the Robert Trent Jones II who was a world-renowned golf course designer.

MAY 9. 2017 TUESDAY

2017.5

农历丁酉年四月

9

十四　周二

宝山烈士陵园

Baoshan District Martyrs Cemetery

宝山区宝杨路 599 号
599 Baoyang Road, Baoshan District

宝山区烈士陵园建于 1956 年，安葬 1884 名革命烈士遗骸。辟有纪念馆，陈列着在 1949 年 5 月上海解放战争宝山战斗中英勇牺牲的烈士事迹及遗物。

Built in 1956, Baoshan District Martyrs Cemetery houses the remains of 1884 revolutionary martyrs. A memorial hall collects the exhibition of heroic deeds and relics of the martyrs who died in Baoshan battle of Shanghai liberation war in May 1949.

MAY 10. 2017 WEDNESDAY

2017.5

农历丁酉年四月

10

十五　周三

历史博物馆

History Museum

浦东新区世纪大道 1 号东方明珠零米大厅内
In the Lobby of Oriental Pearl Tower, 1 Century Avenue, Pudong New Area

创建于 1983 年，原名上海历史文物陈列馆。是一座全面反映上海地区历史发展的博物馆。馆藏大量代表上海历史进程的文物和文献，如马家浜文化、崧泽文化、良渚文化遗存等。

Established in 1983, Shanghai History Museum, formerly, Shanghai History and Artefacts Exhibition Hall, is a museum that fully displays the history of Shanghai. The museum houses a great number of cultural relics and literatures representing the historic course of Shanghai, such as the remains of Majiabang Culture, Songze Culture and Liangzhu Culture.

MAY 11. 2017 THURSDAY 2017.5 农历丁酉年四月

11

十六 周四

宏恩医院（华东医院）

Greater El Monte Community Hospital (Hua Dong Hospital)

静安区延安西路 221 号
221 West Yan'an Road, Jing'an District

旧上海租界时期一位无名氏赠给工部局的一家综合性的医院，建于 1926 年。建筑属欧洲文艺复兴样式，设计者是匈牙利籍著名建筑设计师邬达克。市级文物保护单位。

Built in 1926, Greater El Monte Community Hospital was a comprehensive hospital donated by an anonym to the Municipal Council during the public concession period in Shanghai before 1949. It is a historical and cultural site protected at the municipal level.

12

十七　周五

护士节

五角场商圈
Wujiaochang Business Center

杨浦区五角场镇
Wujiaochang Town, Yangpu District

五角场商圈是上海四大城市副中心之一，因地处五条同源大道的起始处得名。该商圈南部为上海十大商业中心之一，中部为知识创新中央社区，北部为高端知识商务中心。

Named for its location at the intersection of five avenues, Wujiaochang is one of the four sub-centers of Shanghai and listed among Shanghai's top ten business centers. Its center is the central community of knowledge innovation; and its northern part is the high-end knowledge business center.

MAY 13. 2017 SATURDAY

2017.5

农历丁酉年四月

13

十八　周六

跑马总会大厦

Race Club Building

黄浦区南京西路 325 号
325 West Nanjing Road, Huangpu District

1954 年 5 月改为上海图书馆

上世纪 30 年代英国新古典主义风格建筑，曾是闻名一时的上海跑马总会，位于今人民广场、人民公园区域。建国后，先后成为上海博物馆、图书馆、美术馆。市级文物保护单位。

This English-style architecture was the famous Shanghai Race Club in the 1930s, and has been the building of Shanghai Museum, Shanghai Library and Shanghai Art Museum successively after 1949. Now it is a historical and cultural site protected at the municipal level.

14

十九 周日

母亲节

上海国际时尚中心
Shanghai Fashion Center

杨浦区杨树浦路 2866 号
No. 2866, Yangshupu Road, Yangpu District

顶级专业秀场、世界顶级品牌发布首选地，亚洲规模最大的时尚中心，上海打造全球“第六时尚之都”目标的承载体。清水红砖建筑既有工业文明的历史沧桑，又融入当代时尚元素。

As a top professional show venue, it is the preferred place for the product release of the world's top brands, the largest fashion center in Asia, and the carrier of Shanghai's objective to become the world's sixth fashion center. The architecture built by red bricks displays the history of industrial civilization and represents modern fashion as well.

MAY 15. 2017 MONDAY

2017.5

农历丁酉年四月

15

二十　周一

步高里
Cite Bourbobne

黄浦区陕西南路 287 弄
Lane 287 South Shaanxi Road, Huangpu District

1930 年 5 月 16 日建成

建于 1930 年，典型的行列式旧式石库门里弄，也是保存得较完整的罕见的整组里弄住宅，共有砖木结构二层石库门建筑 78 幢。著名作家巴金曾寓于此。市级文物保护单位。

Built in 1930, Cite Bourbobne is a typical traditional line-type Shikumen building, and a rare entire group of neighborhood buildings well preserved in Shanghai. It is a heritage site under municipal protection.

16

廿一 周二

提篮桥监狱

Tilanqiao Prison

虹口区长阳路 147 号
47 Changyang Road., Hongkou District

1903 年 5 月 18 日第一幢监楼启用

中国迄今仍在使用的历史最悠久的监狱。由于建筑精良、规模宏大，提篮桥监狱曾号称“远东第一监狱”。其中一幢楼被建成上海监狱陈列馆。全国重点文物保护单位。

It is the most long-standing prison in China that is still in operation. Because of its magnificent and exquisite buildings, Tilanqiao Prison was once known as the “No.1 Prison in the Far East”. Shanghai Prison Museum is constructed on the former site of the prison. It is an important heritage site under state protection.

17

廿二 周三

上海博物馆

Shanghai Museum

黄浦区人民大道 201 号
201 People Avenue, Huangpu District

大型古代艺术博物馆，中国四大博物馆之一。馆藏自旧石器时代迄近代和现代珍贵文物 14 万件，其陶瓷器、历代书画收藏，有江南半壁江山之说。国家 4A 景区。

It is a large museum of ancient Chinese art and one of the four major museums in China. It has a collection of 140,000 pieces of precious cultural relics ranging from the Paleolithic Age to modern and contemporary times. Legend has it that the chinaware, calligraphy and painting works of different dynasties in its collection account for half of those across South China. It is a 4A-rated national tourist attraction.

MAY 18. 2017 THURSDAY

2017.5

农历丁酉年四月

18

廿三　周四

国际博物馆日

紫海鹭缘浪漫庄园

Purple Egret Lavender Garden

崇明区中部北沿公路 2018 号
2018 North High Way, central part of Chongming District

每年 5 月 20 日至 6 月 20 日薰衣草节

庄园景区内集生态观光、度假旅游、康复疗养、参与性娱乐等多功能为一体，向游客提供“回归大自然”的体验。

Boasting the field scenery, the park integrates the functions of ecological sightseeing, vacation tour, rehabilitation and participatory activities, making it a natural paradise for tourists.

19

廿四 周五

同济大学

Tongji University

杨浦区四平路 1239 号
1239 Siping Road, Yangpu District

5 月 20 日校庆日

前身是 1907 年创办的德文医学堂，1923 年正式定名，是国内以土木建筑学科著称，兼有理、工、医、文、法五大学院的综合性大学。知名校友有乔石、万钢、李国豪等。

Tongji University is a Project 985 and Project 211 university in China under direct administration of the Ministry of Education. It is also one of Chinese universities with the most rigorous standards of admission.

MAY 20. 2017 SATURDAY

2017.5

农历丁酉年四月

20

廿五　周六

崧泽古文化遗址
Songze Ancient Cultural Relic

青浦区城东崧泽村
Songze Village, Chengdong, Qingpu District

1961 年 5 月 21 日第一次发掘

上海地区迄今为止最早的古文化遗址，是崧泽文化的命名地，它的发现为研究太湖地区原始文化和上海史前历史提供了重要的实物资料。全国重点文物保护单位。

It is the earliest ancient cultural relic to date in Shanghai region and where Songze culture gets its name from. It provides important physical materials for studying the primitive culture of the Lake Tai region and the prehistoric history of Shanghai. It is an important heritage site under state protection.

MAY 21. 2017 SUNDAY

2017.5

农历丁酉年四月

21

廿六　周日

小满

大自然野生昆虫馆

Natural Wild Insect Kingdom

浦东新区丰和路 1 号
1 Fenghe Road, Pudong New Area

5 月 22 日世界生物多样性日

集旅游、观赏、科普教育为一体的国内首家活体昆虫展示馆。馆内分区有: 昆虫长廊、蝴蝶谷、两栖爬虫溶洞区、生态触摸区、水域触摸区、热带雨林区、昆虫沙龙及科普教室。

Shanghai Natural Wild Insect Kingdom is China's first live insects exhibition hall, which integrates tourism, appreciation and science education. The exhibition hall is divided into Insect Gallery, Butterfly Valley, Cavern Zone of Amphibians, Ecological Area, Waters Area, Tropical Rain Forest Area, Insect Salon and Science Education Room.

22

廿七　周一

上海大学
Shanghai University

宝山区上大路 99 号
99 Shangda Road, Baoshan District

5 月 27 日校庆日

创建于 1922 年，首任校长于右任。1994 年组建新的上海大学。现为以人文社科见长，涵盖理工、管理、艺术诸多学科的综合性大学。知名校友有费孝通、李硕勋、钱伟长、徐匡迪等。

Shanghai University is a Project 211 key university under the administration of Shanghai jointly established by the Ministry of Education and Shanghai municipal government. There is a saying in history that Peking University is the main front during the May 4th Movement of 1919, and Shanghai University is the main front during the Great Revolution.

23

廿八 周二

圣三一基督教堂（黄浦区政府礼堂）

Holy Trinity Cathedral (Government Hall of Huangpu District)

黄浦区九江路 211 号
211 Jiujiang Road, Huangpu District

1866 年 5 月 24 日开建

上海开埠早期最大最华丽的基督教堂，红砖砌筑，俗称“红礼拜堂”，专门为英国侨民中的圣公会教徒服务。其钟楼长期是上海最醒目的地标和制高点。市级文物保护单位。

Once a church dedicated to the Anglicans in British nationals in Shanghai, it was also the largest and most magnificent Christian church during the early period of Shanghai's opening to the outside world. It is a heritage site under municipal protection.

MAY 24. 2017 WEDNESDAY

2017.5

农历丁酉年四月

24

廿九 周三

东海大桥
Donghai Bridge

浦东新区芦潮港镇
Luchaogang Town, Pudong New Area

2005 年 5 月 25 日通车

上海第一座真正意义上的外海跨海大桥。上海国际航运中心重要组成部分，全长 32.5 公里，其建成通车为上海建设国际航运中心奠定了硬件基础。

It is Shanghai's first cross-sea bridge in the open sea in the true sense and also constitutes an integral part of Shanghai International Shipping Center. With a total length of 32.5 km, it is the "No.1 Project" of the municipal government, laying a hardware foundation for Shanghai to build the international shipping center after it was completed and open to traffic.

MAY 25. 2017 THURSDAY

2017.5

农历丁酉年四月

25

三十 周四

复旦大学
Fudan University

杨浦区邯郸路 220 号
220 Handan Road., Yangpu District

5 月 27 日校庆

中国人自主创办的第一所高等学校，1905 年由教育家马相伯创办，首任校董孙中山。校名取《尚书》名句“日月光华，旦复旦兮”，是以文科为特色的文理医工综合性研究型大学。

Founded in 1905, initiated by the famous educator Mr. Ma Xiangbo, Fudan University is the first tertiary school independently established in China. The school's name originated from "The Book of History",which could be interpreted as the "Sun and the Moon's brilliance renews everyday and never fades". It is now developped into a world renown comprehensive and research type university, majoring on liberal and arts, in addition to science, engineering and medicine specialities.

26

初一　周五

公共租界工部局大楼

The Building of Shanghai Municipal Council

黄浦区江西中路 209–215 号
209–215 Central Jiangxi Road, Huangpu District

1949 年 5 月 27 日上海解放，上海市人民政府、上海市军事管制委员会在此宣告成立

旧上海公共租界最高行政机构工部局的办公大楼，俗称“石头房子”。建筑风格包括古典主义、巴洛克和文艺复兴多种式样。建国伊始为市政府所在地。市级文物保护单位。

Commonly known as the “Stone House”, the building was the office building of Municipal Council, the highest administration authority of public concession in Shanghai before 1949. It is a historical and cultural site protected at the municipal level.

MAY 27. 2017 SATURDAY

2017.5

农历丁酉年五月

27

初二　周六

西康公园

Xikang Park

静安区西康路 255 号
255 Xikang Road, Jing'an District

1951 年 5 月 28 日对外开放

1951 年建成开放。公园呈长方形，种植广玉兰、香樟、雪松、茶花、紫藤、瓜子黄杨等乔灌木。东侧花架炎夏季节浓荫蔽日。园西部有长廊及凉亭。

Xikang Park was completed and opened to public in 1951. Such trees and shrubs as Magnolia grandiflora, Cinnamomum camphora, deodar, camellia, Chinese wisteria and Buxus sinica are planted in this rectangular park. The reinforced concrete flower shelves stand in the east, forming shade in the hot summer. In the west, there are corridors and pavilions.

MAY 28. 2017 SUNDAY

2017.5

农历丁酉年五月

28

初三　周日

宋庆龄陵园

Soong Ching-Ling Mausoleum

长宁区宋园路 21 号
21 Songyuan Road, Changning District

1997 年 5 月 29 日宋庆龄逝世

前身为上海市万国公墓，宋庆龄先生安葬于此。由宋庆龄纪念设施、名人墓园等四个部分组成，环境优美自然，气氛庄严肃穆。全国重点文物保护单位。

It was formerly known as Shanghai International Cemetery where Soong Ching-Ling was buried. It consists of four parts, including Soong Ching-Ling memorial facilities and celebrity cemetery. In the mausoleum, the environment is beautiful and It is an important heritage site under state protection.

MAY 29. 2017 MONDAY

2017.5

农历丁酉年五月

29

初四　周一

美兰湖
Meilan Lake

宝山区沪太路 6688 号（内美兰湖路 10 号）
6688 Hutai Road, Baoshan District (10, Inner Meilan Lake Road)

端午节举办龙舟节

面积 110 亩，是上海市区第二大人工湖、罗店新镇的核心景观，环湖为北欧风情小镇、大型户外公园，被誉为“北上海最美丽的地方”。

Covering an area of 110 mu, it is the second largest artificial lake in Shanghai and the core landscape in Luodian New Town. Around the lake lie a Nordic-style town and a large outdoor park, which are known as the “most beautiful places in the north Shanghai.”.

MAY 30. 2017 TUESDAY

2017.5

农历丁酉年五月

30

初五　周二

端午节

儿童博物馆
Children's Museum

长宁区宋园路 61 号
61 Songyuan Road, Changning District

1996 年儿童节前开放

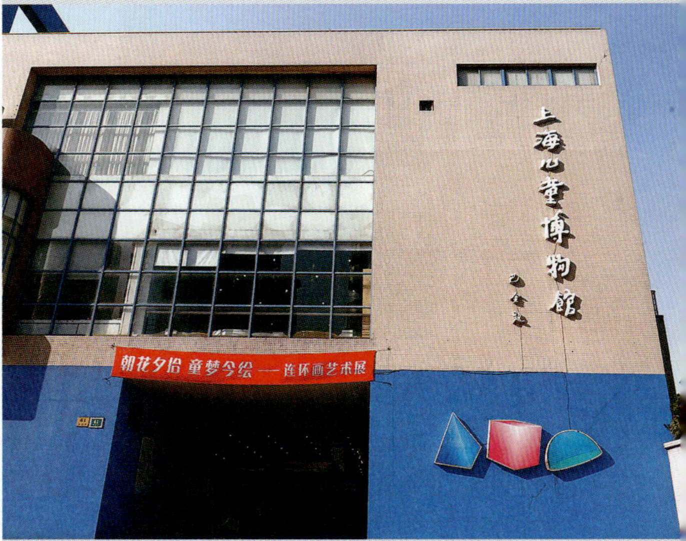

为实现宋庆龄先生“把最宝贵的东西给予儿童”的愿望而建。坐落在宋庆龄陵园东南部，由航天馆、航海馆、玩具馆等组成，调动儿童的五大感官，去认识和探索周围的世界。

Located in the southeast of the Soong Ching-ling Cemetery, it was built for fulfilling her wish of “giving of the most precious to the children”. Composed of the Space Hall, Maritime Hall, Toy Hall, etc., the museum can fully mobilize children's five senses to explore the world around them.

31

初六　周三

世界无烟日

影像·中国
上海地标
2017
OLYMPUS
Canon

陆
June
月
Gillette
Coca-Cola

中国福利会少年宫

The Mansion of Sir Ellis Kadoorie(China Welfare Institute Children's Palace).

静安区延安西路 64 号
64 West Yan'an Road, Jing'an District

全国第一家少年宫。宋庆龄先生于 1953 年创办，馆舍前身是英籍犹太人嘉道理爵士住宅，仿欧洲宫廷建筑，全部使用大理石作为建材，称“大理石宫”。市级文物保护单位。

This former private residence of Sir Ellis Kadoorie, a British Jewish businessman, is also called the "Marble Palace" as the whole body of the building is built of marble. It is a historical and cultural site protected at the municipal level.

JUN. 1. 2017 THURSDAY

2017.6

农历丁酉年五月

1

初七　周四

儿童节

王伯群住宅（长宁区少年宫）

Wang Boqun's Residence(Changning Children's Palace)

长宁区愚园路 1136 弄 31 号
31 Lane 1136 Yuyuan Road, Changning District

意大利哥特式城堡建筑，四层钢筋混凝土结构，各种大小厅室共 32 间。传闻系民国政要王伯群于 1934 年为娶大夏大学校花保志宁所建，旧上海少见之豪宅。市级文物保护单位。

Wang Boqun's Residence is a Gothic castle style building built by Wang Boqun, a politician and Minister of Transportation of the Republic of China, in 1934. It is a heritage site under municipal protection.

2

初八 周五

昆虫博物馆

Entomological Museum C.A.S.

徐汇区枫林路 300 号
300 Fenglin Road, Xuhui District

大型专业昆虫馆。全国青少年科技教育基地。收藏全国各地昆虫标本 100 多万号，保藏一大批濒危珍稀昆虫标本及全世界危险性检疫害虫标本。

It is a large specialized entomological museum and one of national science education bases for teenagers. Through over one hundred years of venture and development, the museum has a collection of more than one million insect specimens from all over the world, and a large collection of rare and precious insect specimens and dangerous quarantine pest specimens across the world.

JUN. 3. 2017 SATURDAY

2017.6

农历丁酉年五月

3

初九　周六

自然博物馆

Natural History Museum

静安区山海关路 399 号
399 Shanhaiguan Road, Jing'an District

中国最大、最古老的自然博物馆之一。迄今已有近 150 年馆史，现为上海科技馆自然分馆，收藏标本近 27 万件。其中“黄河古象”和“马门溪恐龙”是镇馆之宝。

Shanghai Natural History Museum (now a branch of the Shanghai Science and Technology Museum) is one of the largest and oldest museums of natural sciences in China. Up to now, it has a history of nearly 150 years. The museum has a collection of nearly 270,000 samples, with the “Yellow River mammoth” and “Dinosaur Skeleton of Mamenchisaurus Hochuanensis” as the treasure of museum.

4

初十　周日

前卫生态村
Qianwei Ecological Village

崇明区大新镇前卫村
Qianwei Village, Daxin Town, Chongming District

上海市郊最早发展农家乐旅游的村庄之一，也是崇明最出名的农家乐聚集地。村内各项设施完善，田园诗意、有机食品和清洁空气最为引人入胜。国家 4A 景区。

It is among the first villages in the suburb of Shanghai that develop agritainment and also the most famous agritainment base in Chongming. It has complete facilities as well as an attractive countryside lifestyle, organic food and clean air. It is a 4A-rated national tourist attraction.

5

十一　周一

世界环境日　芒种

金山城市沙滩

Jinshan City Beach

金山区石化街道新城路 5 号
5 Xincheng Road, Shihua Subdistrict, Jinshan District

长三角最具有海派风格的城市海岸景观。定期举办系列文化体育赛事，如：排球、足球、模特大赛、音乐节等，成为金山海岸线的名片。国家 4A 景区。

It provides a city coastal landscape that is most typical of Shanghai in the Yangtze Delta, and regularly holds cultural and sports events such as volleyball, soccer, model contests, and music festivals, making it a name card along Jinshan coastline. It is a 4A-rated national tourist attraction.

6

十二　周二

外滩源

Wai Tan Yuan

黄浦区中山东一路 33 号
33, No.1 East Zhongshan Road, Huangpu District

2002 年 6 月 7 日外滩源项目启动

位于黄浦江和苏州河交汇处、外滩历史文化风貌区的核心地带，称为外滩“万国建筑博览会”的源头、上海现代化的起点、上海“皇冠”上的“明珠”。

Located at the intersection of the Huangpu River and the Suzhou River and in the core of historic and cultural scene area of the Bund, it is the source of the “Exhibition of World Architecture” of the Bund, the starting point of Shanghai’s modernization and the “Pearl” of the “Imperial Crown” of Shanghai.

7

十三　周三

长风公园 · 长风海洋世界

Changfeng Park & Changfeng Ocean World

普陀区大渡河路 189 号
189 Daduhe Road, Putuo District

6 月 8 日世界海洋日

上海市大型综合性山水公园，园内长风海洋世界集大型海洋动物表演与水族馆鱼类展览为一体，展出海洋生物 300 多种、1 万多尾 (只)。国家 4A 景区。

It is a large comprehensive landscape park in Shanghai. Inside the park, Changfeng Ocean World holds large marine animal shows and aquarium fish exhibitions with over 10,000 marine animals of over 300 species. It is a 4A-rated national tourist attraction.

8

十四 周四

志丹苑元代水闸遗址

Yuan Dynasty Water Gate Site in Zhidan Garden

普陀区志丹路和延长西路交接处
intersection of Zhidan Road and West Yanchang Road, Putuo District

上海境内研究中国古代水利和海岸水利工程的重要遗存，目前发现的唯一一座元代水闸，做工精致、保存完善，建造方法符合宋代《营造法式》。全国重点文物保护单位。

It is an important historical site in Shanghai for studying ancient hydraulic engineering and costal hydraulic engineering projects of China. It is the only water gate of the Yuan Dynasty discovered to date. The well-preserved water gate demonstrates exquisite workmanship and the construction skills described in Yingzao Fashi, a book about construction skills of the Song Dynasty. It is an important heritage site under state protection.

JUN. 9. 2017 FRIDAY

2017.6

农历丁酉年五月

9

十五　周五

上海图书馆

Shanghai Library

徐汇区淮海中路 1555 号
1555 Middle Huaihai Road, Xuhui District

中国十大图书馆之一，大型综合性研究型公共图书馆。馆藏文献达 5095 万册（件），以历史文献最具特色。新馆多维台阶式块体顶部造型如台阶，象征着文化积淀和新知探索。

As one of China's ten major libraries,Shanghai Library is a public library famous for its social contribution as a comprehensive and research unit. The library's collection amounts to near 51million copies/pieces in both variety and quantity, characteristic of the history collections. Its new venue's roof takes the shape of multidimensional steps symbolizing cultural accumulation and knowledge seeking.

JUN. 10. 2017 SATURDAY

2017.6

农历丁酉年五月

10

十六　周六

宝山国际民间艺术博览馆
Baoshan International Folk Arts Exposition

宝山区顾村镇沪太路 4788 号
4788 Hutai Road, Gucun Town, Baoshan District

6 月 11 日 世界文化遗产日

上海第一家融非物质文化遗产的展示、研究和保护为一体的博览馆，也是目前国内规模最大的世界非物质文化遗产展览馆。享有“文化大观园”之誉。国家 4A 景区。

It is the first exposition in Shanghai that displays, studies and protects intangible cultural heritage, and the largest showplace up to date, on a national basis, for the exhibition of global intangible cultural heritage. It is known as the “Museum of Culture”. It is a 4A-rated national tourist attraction.

11

十七　周日

武康路
Wukang Road

徐汇区
in Xuhui District

原名福开森路，以美国传教士约翰・福开森命名，1907 年法租界公董局修筑，被誉为浓缩了上海百年历史的“名人路”。文化部与国家文物局批准的“中国历史文化名街”。

Wukang Road, formerly known as “Route Ferguson”, was named after American Missionary John Calvin Ferguson. Built by the French Concession in 1907, it is reputed as “Road of Celebrity” that concentrates the one-hundred-year history of Shanghai. It has been rated as a “National Historic and Cultural Street of China” by the Ministry of Culture and State Administration of Cultural Heritage.

12

十八　周一

上海世博会博物馆

World Expo Museum

黄浦区蒙自路 823 号
823 Mengzi Road, Huangpu District

迄今世界范围内唯一一个关于世博会的博物馆。由旧厂房改建，设三个展厅，分别展示世博会 150 多年的史诗、历届世博会精彩作品，以及申办、参与和运筹世博会的内容等。

It is the only Expo themed museum so far on Earth converted from old plants, consists of three exhibition halls, demostrating Expo's 150 years' glorious epics, marvellous creations of its successive events, and others content relating to Expo bidding, participation and operation.

JUN. 13. 2017 TUESDAY　　*2017.6*　　农历丁酉年五月

13

十九　周二

吴淞炮台湾湿地森林公园·长江河口科技馆

Wu Song Pao Tai Wetland Forest Park & Yangtze Estuary Science and Technology Museum

宝山区塘后路 206 号
206 Tanghou Road, Baoshan District

上海唯一一座依山傍海的公园。集科普教育、休闲娱乐、观光旅游等功能于一体、野趣与人文相映的大型公园，内有长江河口科技馆。国家 4A 景区。

It is the only park in Shanghai that sits adjacent to both mountains and the ocean. It is also a large park that integrates the functions of science promotion and education, leisure and entertainment, and sightseeing and tourism, and combines the nature and human culture. Yangtze Estuary Science and Technology Museum is built inside the park. It is a 4A-rated national tourist attraction.

14

二十 周三

汽车博物馆

Auto Museum

嘉定区安亭镇博园路 7565 号
7565 Boyuan Road, Anting Town, Jiading District

中国首个专业汽车博物馆。展示了汽车诞生以来的近 70 辆经典车型，时间跨度逾百年。由历史馆、技术馆、品牌馆、古董车馆和临展馆五部分组成。

The Shanghai Auto Museum is China's first specialized auto museum and features a display of about nearly 70 classic automobiles since the birth of automobile, spanning a time of over one hundred years. It consists of five pavilions: History Pavilion, Technology Pavilion, Brand Pavilion, Antique Car Pavilion and Temporary Exhibition Pavilion.

JUN. 15. 2017 THURSDAY 2017.6 农历丁酉年五月

15

廿一 周四

上海迪斯尼
Shanghai Disneyland

浦东新区川沙新镇
Chuansha New Town , Pudong New Area

2016 年 6 月 16 日正式开业

中国大陆首座迪士尼主题乐园，是一座神奇王国风格的迪士尼主题乐园，包含六个主题园区：米奇大街、奇想花园、探险岛、宝藏湾、明日世界、梦幻世界。

The first Disneyland park in China's Mainland. It is a Magic-Kingdomstyle Disneyland consisting of six themed lands: Mickey Avenue, Gardens of Imagination, Adventure Isle, Treasure Cove, Tomorrowland and Fantasyland.

16

廿二　周五

尚嘉中心

L'Avenue Shanghai

长宁区仙霞路 99 号
99 Xianxia Road, Changning District

2013 年 6 月 17 日开业

位于上海虹桥商圈的时尚生活地标。2013 年开业，是精品业巨舰 LVMH 集团旗下力作，汇聚了大量世界一线品牌和时尚产品。建筑设计独创，出自日本名建筑设计师青木淳的手笔。

Opened in 2013, it is a landmark of fashionable life located at Hongqiao Business Center of Shanghai. As a masterpiece of boutique giant LVMH Group, it gathers a number of world's first-class brands and fashion. The unique architectural design is completed by Jun Aoki, a famous Japanese architectural designer.

JUN. 17. 2017 SATURDAY

2017.6

农历丁酉年五月

17

廿三　周六

瞿秋白寓所旧址

Former Residence of Qu Qiubai

虹口区山阴路 133 弄 12 号
12 Lane 133, Shanyin Road, Hongkou District

1935 年 6 月 18 日瞿秋白牺牲

中共早期主要领导人之一瞿秋白同志生前在上海最后一处寓所。寓所建筑结构保存完好。市级文物保护单位。

It is the last residence of Qu Qiubai, one of the primary leaders of CPC in its early period, in Shanghai. The architectural structure of the residence is well preserved. It is a heritage site under municipal protection.

18

廿四 周日

父亲节

中共“六大”后中央政治局机关旧址

Former Office Site of the Political Bureau of the CPC Central Committee after the 6th National Congress of CPC

黄浦区云南中路 171–173 号
171–173 Middle Yunnan Road, Huangpu District

1928 年 6 月 18 日至 7 月 11 日中共六大召开

1928 年在上海留守的中共中央以“福兴布庄”名义设立的中央政治局机关所在地，是一幢 4 层米色小楼。1931 年因顾顺章叛变，这里停止办公。市级文物保护单位。

As a historical and cultural site protected at the municipal level, the building is the location of the former office of the Political Bureau of the CPC Central Committee established by CPC Central Committee staying back in Shanghai in the name of Fuxing Cloth Store in 1928.

JUN. 19. 2017 MONDAY

2017.6

农历丁酉年五月

19

廿五　周一

1927 年中共江苏省委旧址

Former Site of the CPC Jiangsu Provincial Committee in 1927

虹口区山阴路（恒丰里）69 弄 90 号
90 Lane 69, Shanyin Road (Hengfeng Lane), Hongkou District

1927 年 6 月为省委机关驻地

1927 年大革命失败后，中共新成立的江苏省委机关所在地，是一座坐北朝南砖木结构的三层住宅。市级文物保护单位。

It is where the newly established organ of CPC Jiangsu Provincial Committee was located after the Great Revolution failed in 1927. Being a three-story south-facing residence with a brick-wooden structure, it is a heritage site under municipal protection.

JUN. 20. 2017 TUESDAY

2017.6

农历丁酉年五月

20

廿六　周二

瑞金二路 118 号住宅（瑞金宾馆 1 号楼）

Residence at No. 118 Ruijin Rd.（No.2）(Building 1 of Ruijin Hotel)

黄浦区瑞金二路 118 号
118 No.2 Ruijin Road, Huangpu District

英国古典式府邸，最初是旧上海“冒险家”英国人马立斯的别墅，建于 1917 年。建筑采用红瓦屋顶，有主楼和辅楼，均为两层。建国后为国宾馆。市级文物保护单位。

This two-storied villa of British neoclassical architectural style is also known as Ma Lisieux Villa. It is a heritage site under municipal protection.

21

廿七 周三

夏至

崇明学宫

Chongming Palace of Learning

崇明区城桥镇鳌山路 669 号
669 Aoshan Road, Chengqiao Town, Chongming District

庙（孔庙）学合一的建筑群，始建于元朝泰定年间，是上海仅存的三座学宫之一，现为崇明博物馆馆舍所在地，是一处重要的人文旅游景点。市级文物保护单位。

It is a building cluster where the temple (Confucius Temple) and learning blend. Built during the Taiding period of the Yuan Dynasty, it is one of the three palaces of learning remaining in Shanghai and where Chongming Museum is located. It is a heritage site under municipal protection.

22

廿八　周四

奉城老街

Fengcheng Old Street

奉贤区奉城镇
Fengcheng Town, Fengxian District

相传孔子弟子子游曾到此，故得奉贤县名，清雍正至民国初年奉城为县城。老街呈十字形，有东街、南街、西街、北街，现存奉城古城墙、万佛阁等古迹。

It was said that the disciple of Confucius Ziyou visited here, so the county was named as Fengxian County. From Qing Emperor Yongzheng to the early Republic of China, Fengcheng was a county. The old street of cross shape, is composed of East Street, South Street, West Street and North Street. Now the ancient walls of Fengcheng, Wanfo Temple and other historical sites are well preserved.

23

廿九　周五

国际奥林匹克日

上海古城墙和大境道观

Ancient City Wall and Dajing Taoist Temple

黄浦区大境路 269 号
269 Dajing Road, Huangpu District

由明代古城墙和建在古城墙上的大境道观（关帝庙）组成。据考为明朝嘉靖年间为抗御倭寇侵扰所建的旧上海县古城墙残存的一部分。市级文物保护单位。

It consists of the ancient city wall built in the Ming Dynasty and Dajing (Taoist) Temple built on the ancient city wall. It is reported that it is part of the residual old city wall of Shanghai County in old times built during the Jiajing period of the Ming Dynasty to fend against Japanese attackers. It is a heritage site under municipal protection.

JUN. 24. 2017 SATURDAY

2017.6

农历丁酉年六月

24

初一　周六

多伦路
Duolun Road

虹口区
in Hongkou District

上海最具人文气质的马路，保存了上世纪二三十年代上海的人文风情，众多名人故居及各种民间收藏馆、展览馆、古玩字画等，形成了典雅的文化品位和独特的文博景观。

Duolun road, a road with the most humane qualities in Shanghai, reproduces the cultures and heritages in the 1920s-30s. A number of folk galleries, exhibition halls, antiques, calligraphy and paintings have formed the unique relics and an elegant cultural taste and a museum landscape.

JUN. 25. 2017 SUNDAY

2017.6

农历丁酉年六月

25

初二　周日

嘉定博物馆

Jiading Museum

嘉定区博乐路 215 号
215 Bole Road, Jiading District

2013 年 6 月 26 日新馆开馆

利用孔庙古建筑群作为馆舍，有《嘉定竹刻工艺》等基本陈列室和专题展览室等，展出文物史料 800 余件。旧馆建于 1959 年，新馆 2013 年建成开放。国家二级博物馆。

With the ancient buildings of Confucius Temple as the premises, Jiading Museum has the basic showroom and special exhibition rooms such as the "Jiading Bamboo Craft", displaying more than 800 pieces of historical relics. It is a Grade-Two national museum.

26

初三 周一

上海体育场
Shanghai Stadium

徐汇区天钥桥路 666 号
666 Tianyaoqiao Road, Xuhui District

又称“八万人体育场”。规模和设施仅次于北京的国家体育场，是上海标志性景观，曾被评为“上海市最佳体育建筑”、“新中国 50 周年上海十大经典建筑金奖”等。

Shanghai Stadium (also known as the “80,000-seat Stadium”) features the scale and facilities only next to the Beijing National Stadium. As a landmark landscape of Shanghai, it was rated as the “Best Sports Building in Shanghai” and won the “Gold Prize for Shanghai Top 10 Classical Buildings at the 50th Anniversary of the New China” and other awards.

JUN. 27. 2017 TUESDAY

2017.6

农历丁酉年六月

27

初四　周二

卢浦大桥

Lupu Bridge

黄浦区鲁班路 909 号
909 Luban Road, Huangpu District

2003 年 6 月 28 日建成通车

世界第二长的钢结构拱桥，也是世界上首座完全采用焊接工艺连接的大型拱桥，有“世界第一拱”美称。巨弓般的拱肋顶端设有观光平台，游客可沿拱肋的斜坡台阶步行观光。

Reputed as “the World’s No. 1 Arch Bridge”, it is the world’s second longest arch bridge of steel structure and also the world’s first large arch bridge connected with welding process. A sightseeing platform stands on the top of arch rib like a great bow. The tourists may go sightseeing by walking along the slope steps of the arch rib.

28

初五　周三

大金山岛
Grand Jinshan Island

金山区金山石化海滨以南约 6.6 公里处杭州湾海上
in the Hangzhou Bay, 6.6 km south of the Jinshan Beach, Jinshan District

上海市最大的基岩型海岛，平面略呈菱形，面积 0.229 平方公里，主峰高 103.4 米，上海地面最高点。岛上岩石裸露，岛坡陡峭，岛顶植被茂盛，岛岸为砾滩。

The diamond-shaped island is the biggest bedrock island in Shanghai with the main peak as high as 103.4 m and a covering area of 0.229 km^2. It is the highest point above ground in Shanghai. On the island are steep hills, flourishing vegetation and shingle beaches.

29

初六　周四

国家会展中心
National Exhibition and Convention Center

青浦区盈港东路 168 号
168 East Yinggang Road, Qingpu District

2014 年 6 月 30 日 A、B 馆交付

2014 年由商务部和上海市合作共建的世界上面积最大的建筑单体和会展综合体，位于虹桥商务区核心区西部，由展览场馆、配套商业中心、配套办公楼和配套酒店四大部分构成，形状如四叶草。

Located in the west of the core center of Hongqiao Central Business District, NECC is the largest single block building and exhibition complex in the world. It was jointly built by the Ministry of Commerce of China and Shanghai Municipal Government in 2014. With a clover-shaped exterior, it consists of four main parts: exhibition halls, supporting commercial centers, office buildings, and hotels.

30

初七　周五

影像·中国
上海地标
2017

柒
July
月

中共一大会址纪念馆

Museum of the First National Congress of the Chinese Communist Party

黄浦区兴业路 76 号
76 Xingye Road, Huangpu District

1921 年 7 月 1 日中国共产党成立

中国共产党诞生地。中共一大旧址纪念馆，于 1999 年 5 月 27 日上海解放 50 周年纪念日竣工并正式对外开放，为砖木结构、中西合璧式的石库门楼房。全国重点文物保护单位。

It is the birthplace of the Communist Party of China. It was completed and opened on May 27, 1999, the 50th anniversary of the liberation of Shanghai. The museum is a brick-wooden Shikumen structure combining Chinese and Western elements. It is an important heritage site under state protection.

JUL. 1. 2017 SATURDAY

2017.7

农历丁酉年六月

1

初八　周六

建党日

中共中央上海局机关旧址

Former Office Site of Shanghai Bureau of CPC Central Committee

长宁区江苏路 389 弄 21 号
21 Lane 389, Jiangsu Road, Changning District

解放战争期间党中央派驻国统区的党组织——中共中央上海局机关所在地，为砖木结构假四层，联列式。旧址再现当年原貌，陈列有相关珍贵展品。市级文物保护单位。

The original look of Shanghai Bureau of CPC Central Committee, the CPC organization dispatched by CPC Central Committee in Kuomintang areas during China's War of Liberation is reproduced with relevant precious exhibits displayed. It is now a municipality protected historic and cultural site.

JUL. 2. 2017 SUNDAY

2017.7

农历丁酉年六月

2

初九　周日

东方艺术中心
Oriental Art Center

浦东新区丁香路 425 号
425 Dingxiang Road, Pudong New Area

2005 年 7 月正式运营

上海的标志性文化设施。曾入选“上海十大时尚地标”。外形宛若一朵美丽的“蝴蝶兰”。国内首家举办过柏林爱乐乐团与维也纳爱乐乐团世界两大顶尖乐团音乐会的剧场。

Shanghai Oriental Art Center, a landmark cultural facility of Shanghai, was elected as one of “Shanghai Top 10 Fashion Landmarks”, and it is shaped like a beautiful butterfly orchid in full bloom. It is China’s first theatre to witness the concerts performed by the two world’s leading orchestras: Berliner Philharmoniker and Wiener Philharmoniker.

3

初十　周一

铁路上海南站
Shanghai South Railway Station

徐汇区沪闵路 289 号
289 Humin Road, Xuhui District

2006 年 7 月开通运营

上海第二大火车站、铁路交通的南大门。列车主要发往长江流域、珠江三角洲及中国南方地区，是上海城市总体规划确定的对外交通枢纽和市内换乘枢纽。

As the south gateway of Shanghai railway traffic, Shanghai South Railway Station is the train station with the second largest traffic in Shanghai, and the external transportation hub and the city transfer hub identified in Shanghai Urban Master Plan.

4

十一 周二

马陆葡萄艺术村

Malu Grape Art Village

嘉定区马陆镇大治东路 285 号
285 East Dazhi Road, Malu Town, Jiading District

7 月 5 日 –10 月 7 日葡萄节

素有“全国葡萄之乡”美誉，所产“马陆葡萄”品种有一百多种；村中还有个性突出的画家工作室和画家村，是一个多功能新型农业旅游村。国家 4A 景区。

It has always been reputed as the “Town of Grapes in China” and produces over one hundred species of “Malu” grapes. In the village, there is an artist studio and an artist village with distinctive features. Being a 4A-rated national tourist attraction, it is a new agricultural tourism village with multiple functions.

JUL. 5. 2017 WEDNESDAY　*2017.7*　**农历丁酉年六月**

5

十二　周三

漕河泾新兴技术开发区
Caohejing Hi-Tech Park

徐汇区虹梅路
Hongmei Road, Xuhui District

1984 年 7 月筹建

我国第一批国家级经济技术开发区和高新技术开发区、国家生态工业示范园区。综合经济指标位于全国前列，目前已形成微电子、光电子、计算机机器软件和新材料等四大产业。

Caohejing Hi-Tech Park is one of first national economic & technological development zones and hi-tech development zones, and also one of national ecological industry demonstration parks. With its composite economic indicator ranking top in China, it has formed four major industries, microelectronics, photoelectron, computer & machine software and new materials.

6

十三　周四

八路军驻沪办事处（兼新四军驻沪办事处）旧址

Former Site of the Eight Route Army Shanghai Office (and New Fourth Army Shanghai Office)

静安区延安中路 504 弄 21 号
21 Lane 504 Middle Yan'an Road, Jing'an District

1937 年 7 月 7 日全面抗战开始

国共建立抗日统一战线后，1937 年 8 月八路军（兼新四军）驻沪办事处所在地，直到上海沦陷转入地下。市级文物保护单位。旧址尚未对外开放，仅有铭牌可供拍摄留念。

It is where the Eight Route Army (and New Fourth Army) Shanghai Office was located after CPC and KMT established the anti-Japanese united front and went underground until Shanghai was occupied by the Japanese. It is a heritage site under municipal protection (the former site is not opened yet to the public and there is only a name tablet for taking photos).

7

十四　周五

小暑

玛雅海滩水公园

Playa Maya Waterpark

松江区佘山镇林湖路 888 号
888 Linhu Road, Sheshan Town, Songjiang District

2013 年 7 月初开园，仅夏季开放

上海和华东地区目前最大的露天水上公园。位于上海欢乐谷西南部，占地约 12.8 万平方米。特色项目有双轨磁悬浮水上过山车、章鱼大滑道、魔幻互动超级水寨、深海漩涡体验等。

Located at the Southwest of Shanghai Happy Valley, the Playa Maya Waterpark, covering an area of about 128,000 square meters, is the biggest outdoor waterpark so far in the Eastern China. It offers such featured services as dual-track maglev above-water roller coaster , big octopus slide, interactive magic super water village , and deep-sea whirlpool experience.

JUL. 8. 2017 SATURDAY

2017.7

农历丁酉年六月

8

十五　周六

奉贤华亭东海塘遗址

Relics of Dong Seawall in Huating Town of Fengxian District

奉贤区柘林镇南奉柘公路南侧
South Side of Fengzhe Highway, Zhelin Town, Fengxian District

1712 年 7 月此处海溢成灾

始建于清雍正年间的“石为骨、土为肤”的石质古海塘堤岸，西起今金山区金山嘴，东至奉贤区柘林镇奉海村，全长约 24 公里。市级文物保护单位。

Initially built in the Yongzheng Period of Qing Dynasty, the ancient stone seawall embankment stretches around 24,000 kilometers from Jinshanzui of Jinshan District today in the west to Fenghai Village of Tuolin Town in Fengxian District in the east. It is now a municipality protected historic and cultural site.

9

十六　周日

江湾体育乐园

Jiangwan Sports Center

杨浦区淞沪路 245 号
245 Songhu Road, Yangpu District

大型主题娱乐场所。知名游乐项目有国内规模最大的“造波环流游泳池”，从日本引进的大型三环滑车和沪港合营的 180 度球幕电影。广场上停放着退役的 4 架军用飞机。

It is a large recreation area. The famous recreational programs include domestic largest “wave-making circulation swimming pool”, large three-ring pulley imported from Japan and 180° full dome movie made by a Shanghai-Hong Kong joint venture. Four military airplanes of Air Force stationed in Shanghai park on the square.

JUL. 10. 2017 MONDAY

2017.7

农历丁酉年六月

10

十七　周一

中国航海博物馆

China Maritime Museum

浦东新区新城镇申港大道 197 号
197 Shengang Avenue, Xincheng Town, Pudong New Area

2010 年 7 月 11 日郑和下西洋起锚日开馆

中国第一家国家级航海博物馆，也是中国目前规模最大、等级最高的综合性航海博物馆。国家 4A 景区。

It is the first national maritime museum in China approved by the State of Council, and also the largest comprehensive maritime museum of the highest level in China to date. It is a 4A-rated national tourist attraction.

JUL. 11. 2017 TUESDAY　　2017.7　　农历丁酉年六月

11

十八　周二

爱神花园

Residence of Liu Jisheng

静安区巨鹿路 675 号

675 Julu Road, Jing'an District

上世纪 30 年代建成，当时上海最美丽的花园住宅之一。意大利文艺复兴风格建筑，现为上海市作家协会，上海市标志性文化设施和文学活动中心。

Completed in the 1930s, it was one of the most beautiful garden villas in Shanghai at that time with an Italian Renaissance style. Today it is the home ofShanghai Writers' Association and first-classliterary publications. It has become an iconic cultural facility and a center for literary activities in Shanghai.

JUL. 12. 2017 WEDNESDAY　2017.7　农历丁酉年六月

12

十九　周三

云间第一楼

No. 1 Gate Tower of Yunjian

上海市松江区中山东路 250 号

250 East Zhongshan Road, Songjiang District

云间第一楼原为松江府署谯楼。相传其楼基原是三国时东吴大将陆逊的点将台，古楼清水砖墙，翘角飞逸，古色古香。

It formerly served as the watchtower of Songjiang government. A legend has it that the building's foundation is formerly the call-officers-roll platform of Lu Xun, a senior general of Kingdom of Wu in the Three Kingdoms Period. Featuring double eaves, gable, hip roofs and plain brick walls, the building looks antique and imposing.

13

二十 周四

大世界

Great World Indoor Playground

黄浦区西藏南路 1 号
No.1 South Xizang Road, Huangpu District

1917 年 7 月 14 日开业

旧上海法租界内著名综合性游乐会所，曾被誉为“中国第一俱乐部”、“东方迪斯尼”，是中西结合的塔楼式古典建筑。市级文物保护单位。

Great World Indoor Playground was a famous integrated recreational club in Shanghai before 1949, once known as the “China's First Club” and the “Oriental Disney”. It is a historical and cultural site protected at the municipal level.

JUL. 14. 2017 FRIDAY

2017.7

农历丁酉年六月

14

廿一　周五

南翔檀园

Nanxiang Tanyuan Garden

嘉定区南翔镇混堂弄 5 号
5 Huntang Lane, Nanxiang Town, Jiading District

檀园原为明代文人李流芳的私家园林，因其号檀园，故此得名。全园布局紧凑得体，以葫芦形水池居中，厅堂环立、洞壑盘旋宛转，曲廊贯通全园，体现了江南私家园林的特色。

Tanyuan Garden is originally a private garden of Li Liufang, a scholar in the Ming Dynasty, who styled himself Tanyuan, from which the garden gets its name. The garden is compact and appropriate in its layout, where a central pear-shaped pool is surrounded by halls and roundabout gullies and the zigzag veranda runs through. And all these show the characteristics shared by private gardens in regions south of Yangtze River.

15

廿二　周六

中国共产党第二次全国代表大会会址

Site of the Second National Congress of CPC

静安区成都北路 7 弄 30 号
30 Lane 7 North Chengdu Road, Jing'an District

1922 年 7 月 16 日中共二大召开

中国共产党召开第二次全国代表大会的场所，也是我党第一个出版社人民出版社诞生地。会址纪念馆根据李达及夫人王会悟的回忆布置。全国重点文物保护单位。

It is where the Second National Congress of the CPC was held and the birthplace of the first CPC publishing house — Renmin Press. The museum is furnished according to the memory of Mr. Li Da and his wife Wang Huiwu. It is an important heritage site under state protection.

16

廿三　周日

七宝古镇

Qibao Ancient Town

闵行区七宝镇
Qibao Town, Minhang District

上海四大古镇之一，一座既有江南水乡自然风光，又有悠久人文内涵的历史古镇。风景如画，典型的城中之镇，也是离上海市区最近的古镇。

As one of the four ancient towns in Shanghai, Qibao is a historic town with both natural scenery in the southern region of Yangtze River (or Jiangnan) and time-honored cultural connotations. Being picturesque, it is a typical town within the city, also the nearest ancient town from the Shanghai urban area.

JUL. 17. 2017 MONDAY　　*2017.7*　　农历丁酉年六月

17

廿四　周一

孙科住宅

Sun Ke's Residence

长宁区番禺路 60 号
60 Panyu Road, Changning District

孙中山先生之子孙科在上海的住宅，混合式中西建筑，海派建筑的范例。住宅屋顶、筒瓦、檐口属西班牙建筑风格，外墙面是美国风格，庭园则为中国格式。现为上海生物制品研究所使用。市级文物保护单位。

Sun Ke's Residence is the residence of Mr. Sun Yat-sen's son in Shanghai. This hybrid of Chinese and Western architecture became a Shanghai style architectural paradigm. It is a heritage site under municipal protection.

JUL. 18. 2017 TUESDAY

2017.7

农历丁酉年六月

18

廿五　周二

巨鹿路花园住宅群

Garden Residential Complex at Julu Road

静安区巨鹿路 849-863 号、865 弄和 889-899 号
849-863 Lane 865, 889-899 Julu Road, Jing'an District

位于巨鹿路中段，是租界时代英商亚细亚石油公司于 1929 年为外籍员工建设的大型花园住宅群，砖混结构，占地面积 39 亩。上海市优秀历史建筑。

Located in the middle segment of Julu Road, it is a large-scale garden residential complex of brick-concrete structure, which was built by the British firm Asiatic Petroleum Company for its foreign employees in 1929. Covering an area of 39 mu, it is rated as an excellent historical buildings of Shanghai.

19

廿六　周三

上海虹桥火车站
Shanghai Hongqiao Railway Station

闵行区申贵路 1500 号
1500 Shengui Road, Minhang District

2008 年 7 月 20 日正式开工建设

中国现代化程度最高的铁路客运车站、上海市第一大火车站，是上海虹桥综合交通枢纽的重要组成部分，也是亚洲超大型铁路综合枢纽。2010 年建成启用。

As a highly modernized railway passenger station of China, Shanghai Hongqiao Railway Station is not only an important part of Shanghai Hongqiao integrated transportation hub, but also a ultra-large railway integrated hub in Asia. It was completed and put into service in 2010.

JUL. 20. 2017 THURSDAY

2017.7

农历丁酉年六月

20

廿七　周四

古猗园

Guyi Garden

嘉定区南翔镇沪宜公路 218 号

218 Huyi Highway, Nanxiang Town, Jiading District

7 月 21 日起荷花盛放周

建于明代的江南名园，园内的唐代经幢、宋代石塔、南厅、微音阁等文物是代表传统文化特色的珍品。上海市五大古典园林之一、上海五星级公园、国家 4A 景区。

It is a famous Jiangnan (south China, particularly referring to the downstream region of Yangtze River in ancient China) garden built in the Ming Dynasty. The Buddhist scripture pillars (Jingchuang) built in the Tang Dynasty, stone pagodas built in the Song Dynasty, Southern Hall, Weiyin Pavilion and other cultural sites are treasures representing traditional cultural features. It is one of the five major classical gardens in Shanghai, a five-star park in Shanghai and a 4A-rated national tourist attraction.

JUL. 21. 2017 FRIDAY　　2017.7　　农历丁酉年六月

21

廿八　周五

碧海金沙

Bihai Jinsha

奉贤区海涵路 2 号
2 Haihan Road, Fengxian District

农历大暑日宜前往

目前中国最大的人造沙滩海滨浴场，也是上海唯一一处碧波荡漾的蓝色海域。有上海最大的海上舞台和各类游艺项目，光影水舞数码音乐喷泉也很有特色。国家 4A 景区。

It is currently the largest artificial beach in China and also the only blue sea area in Shanghai where the water is clear enough to swim. It has the largest stage in sea on a municipal basis and various recreation facilities, especially the light-shadow-water dance digital music fountain. It is a 4A-rated national tourist attraction.

22

廿九　周六

大暑

松江佘山九江公路

Jiujiang Road, Sheshan Town, Songjiang District

松江区佘山镇南起沈砖公路，北至后官塘桥
From Shenzhuan Road in the south to Houguantang Bridge in the north. Sheshan Town, Songjiang District

全长 6 公里的郊区公路，或行驶或骑游，两侧为数千亩油菜花田，间嵌着池塘和农家小洋楼，树荫密布，果园成片，有着“春花大道”的美誉。上海最美公路。

The road is 6 km in length in the suburb of Shanghai with thousands of acres of rape flower fields on both sides interlaced with ponds, rural villas, groves, and orchards. You may either drive a car or ride a bicycle to enjoy the beautiful scenery. Renowned as the Road of Blossoms, it is the most beautiful road in Shanghai.

JUL. 23. 2017 SUNDAY　　2017.7　　农历丁酉年闰六月

23

初一　周日

第一次国共合作时期国民党上海执行部旧址

Former Site of KMT Shanghai Office during the First CPC-KMT Cooperation Period

黄浦区南昌路 180 号

180 Nanchang Road, Huangpu District

1924–1926 年间第一次国共合作时期国民党在上海的重要活动场所。是一座坐北朝南，砖木结构西式二层楼房，双坡顶，市级文物保护单位。

It is where important activities of KMT were conductedin Shanghai during the first CPC-KMT cooperation period from1924 to 1926. Being a two-story south-facing building with a brick-wooden structure and a gable roof, it is a heritage site under municipal protection.

JUL. 24. 2017 MONDAY

2017.7

农历丁酉年闰六月

24

初二　周一

明德里
Mingde Lane

黄浦区延安中路 545 弄
Lane 545, Middle Yan'an Road, Huangpu District

在陕西南路、茂名南路之间，1927 年建成，是被列入“里弄住宅风貌街坊”的中心城区新式里弄。

Located between South Shaanxi Road and South Maoming Road, it was completed in 1927 and listed as a new-style lane “with lane and alley residential style “ in the downtown.

25

初三 周二

浦江饭店

Astor House Hotel

虹口区黄浦路 15 号
15 Huangpu Road, Hongkou District

1882 年 7 月 26 日上海首次试燃电灯在此进行

原名礼查饭店，始建于 1846 年，具有新古典主义维多利亚巴洛克式建筑，中国第一家现代化意义上的酒店，让上海走向世界的最初舞台。

Founded in 1846, the Astor House Hotel (formerly known as "the Richards Hotel") is a Neoclassic Victorian baroque style building. It is China's first modern hotel and serves as a window for communication among people of lofty ideas in the East and West and also the initial stage for Shanghai to go global.

JUL. 26. 2017 WEDNESDAY　*2017.7*　农历丁酉年闰六月

26

初四　周三

永嘉庭

Surpass Court

徐汇区永嘉路 570 号
570 Yongjia Road, Xuhui District

位于上海最具有法式风情的使馆区永嘉路上，曾是法租界地，后来为上海航天技术院 808 研究所。现被改造建设成一个集时尚休闲、文化餐饮、创意办公为一体的文创生活空间。

Located on Yongjia Road in the embassy district with the most French style in Shanghai, it was a part of the French Concession and then served as the No.808 Institute of Shanghai Academy of Spaceflight Technology. Now it is built into an elegant space that integrates fashion & leisure, culture, catering and creative office.

27

初五　周四

百乐门

The Paramount

静安区愚园路 218 号
218 Yuyuan Road, Jing'an District

2003 年 7 月 28 日修缮后重新开张

全称“百乐门大饭店舞厅”，以英文名 Paramount Hall 发音得名，是 1932 年中国商人顾联承投资营建，上海著名的综合性娱乐场所。上海市优秀历史建筑。

The Paramount, is “Paramount Dancing Hall” in full. Invested by Chinese merchant Gu Liancheng in 1932, it is a well-known comprehensive place of recreation in Shanghai. It is rated as an excellent historical building in Shanghai.

28

初六　周五

松江清真寺

Songjiang Mosque

松江区缸甏巷 75 号
75 Gangbeng Lane, Songjiang District

原名真教寺，建于元代至正年间，是上海地区最古老、融合中国宫殿式古典风格和阿拉伯建筑风格的伊斯兰教寺院，窑殿和邦克门两处最具特色。市级文物保护单位。

Built during the Zhizheng Period of Yuan Dynasty and formerly called the Real Religion Mosque, Songjiang Mosque is the oldest Islamic building in Shanghai. It is a municipality protected historic and cultural site.

JUL. 29. 2017 SATURDAY

2017.7

农历丁酉年闰六月

29

初七　周六

汾阳路 79 号住宅（上海工艺美术博物馆）

No. 79 Fenyang Road Residence (Shanghai Museum of Arts & Crafts)

徐汇区汾阳路 79 号
79 Fenyang Road, Xuhui District

原为法租界公董局总董官邸，法国后期文艺复兴式建筑，因外墙为白色，故有"海上小白宫"之称。现为上海工艺美术博物馆。市级文物保护单位。

It is the original official residence of the president of the Municipal Council Building of the French Concession. As its facades are white, the building is also called "Little White House in Shanghai". Now the building is used as Shanghai Museum of Arts & Crafts to exhibit the development and history of Shanghai arts and crafts industry. It is now a historical and cultural site protected at the municipal level.

JUL. 30. 2017 SUNDAY

2017.7

农历丁酉年闰六月

30

初八　周日

M50 创意园

M50 Creative Park

普陀区莫干山路 50 号
50 Moganshan Road, Putuo District

2011 年 7 月由春明粗纺厂改建

以“艺术、创意、生活”为核心价值的上海创意产业园区之一，入驻有一大批优质艺术客户，举办过上海国际服装文化节。现为全国工业旅游示范点、“上海十大时尚坐标”。

It is one of the cradles for Shanghai's creative industries with "art, creativity and life" as the core value. A large number of excellent art clients have settled in this Park. Shanghai International Fashion Cultural Festival was held in the Park. Now it is a National Industrial Tourist Demonstration Site and one of Shanghai Top 10 Fashion Coordinates.

31

初九　周一

影像·中国
上海地标
2017
ZEN
SOAHC
川揚名菜
廣式點心
鴻禧茶居

ZEN
采蝶轩
捌
August
月
采蝶轩
ZEN

海军上海博览馆

Navy Shanghai Museum

宝山区吴淞塘后路 68 号
68 Tanghou Road, Wusong, Baoshan District

坐落于长江口的吴淞军港。1991 年创建，主体展览馆是一座宏大的拱形建筑，内设四大展厅，馆藏丰富的海军、海洋历史资料及海军军事装备实物。全国爱国主义教育示范基地。

Navy Shanghai Museum, founded on the year 1991, is located at the Wusong Naval Port, tightly close to the mouth of Yangtze River. The main body of which is an arched building and consists four exhibition halls, demonstrating the history of modern Chinese navy, China's ocean usage and China naval arms' build-up process.The site was appointed as National Patriotic Education Base.

1

初十　周二

建军节

上海当代艺术博物馆

Power Station of Art

黄浦区花园港路 200 号
200 Huayuangang Road, Huangpu District

国内第一家公立当代艺术博物馆。2012 年设立。馆址前身是原南市发电厂、世博会“城市未来馆”。展陈面积达到 1.5 万平方米，拥有 12 个展厅。是上海双年展的所在地。

Established in 2012, the Power Station of Art (PSA) is the first state-run museum dedicated to contemporary art in Chinese Mainland. Renovated from the former Nanshi Power Plant, PSA was once the Pavilion of Future during the 2010 Shanghai World Expo. Covering an exhibition area of 15,000 square meters, PSA has 12 exhibition halls and serves as the venue of Shanghai Biennial.

2

十一　周三

X2 上海数字娱乐中心

X2 Creative Space

徐汇区茶陵北路 20 号
20 North Chaling Road, Xuhui District

2006 年 8 月 3 日创立

以 IT 与创意设计业为主的商业创意产业园区，由上世纪 80 年代老厂房改建而成，有全上海最大的数字音乐酒吧、各种 IT 创意公司、国外风投和文化传播公司等。

X2 Creative Space is a commercial creative industry park specializing in IT and creative designs. Renovated from the old factory building in the 1980s, it gathers Shanghai's largest digital music bar, various IT creative companies, foreign VC firms and cultural communication companies.

3

十二　周四

国际赛车场

International Circuit

嘉定区伊宁路 2000 号
2000 Yining Road, Jiading District

世界一级方程式比赛道之一，也是上海国际汽车城的核心项目。赛道总长度 7 公里左右（包括备用赛道长度），由一级方程式（F1）赛道和其他类型赛道组成。

Shanghai International Circuit is one of the world's first-level formula race tracks and also one of key projects of Shanghai International Automobile City. The race track, totally about seven kilometers long (including the length of alternate race track), consists of Formula 1 (F1) race track and other types of race tracks.

4

十三　周五

西摩会堂
Ohel Rachel Synagogue

静安区陕西北路 500 号
500 North Shaanxi Road, Jing'an District

上海现存时间最早、远东地区规模最大的犹太教会堂，也是上海唯一入选世界纪念性建筑遗产保护名录的建筑。1920 年落成，新古典主义风格，希腊神殿式的长方形的砖木结构。

It is a Jewish synagogue with the longest history and largest scale in the Far East that survives in Shanghai. Completed in 1920 and included in to the List of World Heritage in Commemorationin 2002, it is a neoclassical brick-wood architecture shaped in rectangular of the Greek-temple style.

AUG. 5. 2017 SATURDAY

2017.8

农历丁酉年闰六月

5

十四　周六

动漫艺术馆
Animation & Comics Museum

浦东新区张江路 69 号
69 Zhangjiang Road, Pudong New Area

中国第一家集展示、交流、科普教育、实践互动、产业促进等多功能于一体的大型动漫专业展馆。内设历史展呈馆、互动体验馆、多功能 3D 影院、临展区等，藏品展品逾万件。

It is a large modern professional museum with the integrated functions of display, exchange, science education, practice & interaction, industrial promotion, etc. With the historical exhibition hall, interactive experience hall, multifunctional 3D cinema and temporary exhibition area, the museum has a collection of over 10,000 exhibits.

AUG. 6. 2017 SUNDAY　　2017.8　　农历丁酉年闰六月

6

十五　周日

刘海粟美术馆新馆

Liu Haisu Art Museum (New Building)

长宁区虹桥路 1660 号
No. 1660, Hongqiao Road, Changning District

1994 年 8 月 7 日刘海粟逝世

集美术馆、博物馆和个人纪念馆功能为一体的国家重点美术馆，新馆位于长宁区凯桥绿地东侧，面积是原馆的 3 倍，设计立意为“云海山石”，取意刘海粟一生“为师为友”的黄山。

It is a national key art gallery combining the functions of gallery, museum and personal memorial. The new museum is located in the east of Kaiqiao Green Land in Changning District, covering an area three times as large as the old one. The design is based on the image of “mountain rocks and cloud sea”, inspired by Mount Huang, a lifetime mentor and friend of Mr. Liu Haisu.

7

十六　周一

立秋

自行车主题公园

Bicycle Theme Park

崇明区陈家镇东滩大道
Dongtan Avenue, Chenjia Town, Chongming District

8 月 8 日中国全民健身日

上海首个集休闲、娱乐与运动于一体的郊野主题公园，以自行车文化为主题，强调生态、低碳、休闲的生活方式，是自行车文化集中展示区和体验区。

It is the first theme park integrating leisure, entertainment and sports at the outskirts of Shanghai. Themed with bicycle culture, the Park emphasizes the ecological, low-carbon and leisure lifestyle, becoming a concentrated demonstration and experience area of bicycle culture.

8

十七　周二

青浦奥特莱斯
Bailian Outlets Plaza

青浦区沪青平公路 2888 号
2888 Huqingping Road, Qingpu District

国际时尚风格的大型商业购物城。以销售国际、国内著名品牌折扣服饰和日用品为主，集休闲、餐饮、娱乐等多业态为一体。

It is a large international, modern and fashionable shopping complex that integrates multiple business formats, such as leisure, catering and entertainment, with a focus on selling discount apparels and daily necessities of domestic and foreign famous brands.

9

十八　周三

淀山湖
Dianshan Lake

青浦区城西与江苏省接壤
West to Qingpu District, bordering on Kunshan, Jiangsu Province

上海最大的天然淡水湖泊、黄浦江的源头之一。环湖散落着朱家角古镇、大观园等 5 个国家 4A 景区，是青浦新城的核心景观带，现为国家级水利风景区。

It is the largest natural freshwater lake in Shanghai and also one of the sources of the Huangpu River. Around the lake, there are 5 national 4A-level scenic spots including Zhujiajiao Ancient Town and Grand View Garden. As the core landscape area of Qingpu New City, it is now one of national water conservancy scenic spots.

10

十九 周四

中国劳动组合书记部旧址

Former Site of China Trade Union Secretariat (the museum has been relocated to 1-7 Lane 893)

静安区成都北路 399 号 (陈列馆已移至 893 弄 1–7 号)
399 North Chengdu Road, Jing'an District

1921 年 8 月 11 日劳合成立

中国共产党为加强对工人运动的领导，1921 年 8 月成立中国劳动组合书记部（中华全国总工会的前身），此处为指挥机关所在地。市级文物保护单位。

In August 1921, the CPC established China Trade Union Secretariat (the forerunner of All-China Federation of Trade Unions) to strengthen the leadership over labor movements. This is where the command organs of China Trade Union Secretariat were located. It is a heritage site under municipal protection.

AUG. 11. 2017 FRIDAY

2017.8

农历丁酉年闰六月

11

二十　周五

安福路
Anfu Road

徐汇区
in Xuhui District

8 月 12 日国际青年日

上海最具有文艺范的代表性马路之一，上海话剧艺术中心是文艺青年和艺术发烧友必去之地，西班牙总领事馆以及街角咖啡馆都让这条路文艺味道更为浓厚。

Anfu Road is one of representative roads with the richest ambience of literature and art in Shanghai. Shanghai Dramatic Arts Centre is a place that literary youth and art fans will never miss. The Consulate General of Spain and the cafes around the corner add more charm of literature and art to this road.

AUG. 12. 2017 SATURDAY

2017.8

农历丁酉年闰六月

12

廿一　周六

衡山路

Hengshan Road

徐汇区

in Xuhui District

上海最负盛名的休闲娱乐街，前身为法国公董局 1922 年修筑的贝当路。道路两旁是繁茂的法国梧桐及掩映其中的众多近代优秀建筑，可体验酒吧美食、文艺气息的风情上海。

Hengshan Road, formerly Avenue Petain built by the former French Concession in 1922, is the most famous street for leisure and recreation. There are luxuriant platanus and numerous excellent buildings of the modern times lining the street. It features the experience of bar delicacies and ambience of literature at night.

AUG. 13. 2017 SUNDAY

2017.8

农历丁酉年闰六月

13

廿二　周日

张元济故居

Former Residence of Zhang Yuanji

徐汇区淮海中路 1285 弄 24 号
24 Lane 1285, Middle Huaihai Road, Xuhui District

1959 年 8 月 14 日张元济逝世

中国现代出版家、出版界元老、商务印书馆原董事长张元济在此生活长达 20 年，度过事业上的鼎盛期。是一幢西洋格式布局的三层楼新式里弄房子。市级文物保护单位。

It is the place where Zhang Yuanji, a Chinese modern publisher, a publishing veteran and the former president of the Commercial Press lived for two decades and where he spent the heyday of his career. It is now a municipality protected historic and cultural site.

14

廿三 周一

佘山天主教堂

Sheshan Catholic Church

松江区佘山镇西佘山

West Sheshan Hill, Sheshan Town, Songjiang District

8 月 15 日天主教圣母升天节

著名的中国天主教圣母朝圣地，也是远东第一座受到教宗敕封的圣殿。巴洛克风格建筑，融希腊、罗马、哥特建筑艺术于一炉，部分采用中国传统建筑手法。市级文物保护单位。

Sheshan Catholic Church is not only the famous Marian shrine of Catholic in China, but also the first shrine named by Pope in the Far East. It is now a historical and cultural site protected at the municipal level.

AUG. 15. 2017 TUESDAY

2017.8

农历丁酉年闰六月

15

廿四　周二

新城饭店

Metropole Hotel

黄浦区江西中路 180 号
180 Middle Jiangxi Road, Huangpu District

1930 年由上海犹太协会会长沙逊出资兴建的典型巴洛克风格的半圆凹塔形建筑，在外滩“万国建筑”中独领风骚，其营造的“都会生活”风靡一时。

Metropole Hotel is a semicircle concave-pyramid building of classical Baroque style, invested by President Sassoon of Shanghai Jewish Communal Association in 1930. It's the only one of its kind amid the World Architectures on the Bund, and the “city life” it created was all the rage.

16

廿五 周三

义和坊

Yi He Fang

黄浦区复兴中路 263 弄
Lane 263, Middle Fuxing Road, Huangpu District

见证老上海邻里亲情的石库门建筑。坊内看点是光明托儿所，是独幢三层混合结构的石库门，内部木窗、吊平顶、铁艺都很精致。置拆迁中，涂鸦艺术吸引摄影家纷至沓来。

It is a Shikumen building witnessing the neighborhood affection of Old Shanghai. The highlight is Guangming Nursery, a three-storey independent Shikumen building of composite structure. The interior wood windows, suspended roof and iron art are very exquisite. Now it is subject to relocation, but the graffiti art has attracted many photographers here.

AUG. 17. 2017 THURSDAY　　*2017.8*　　农历丁酉年闰六月

17

廿六　周四

半岛 1919 创意园区
Bund 1919 Cultural Garden Creative Space

宝山区淞兴西路 258 号
258 West Songxing Road, Baoshan District

集聚影视传媒、网游动漫制作等时尚元素的国际创意园，前身是上海第八棉纺织厂，以“老建筑、老厂房、新产业、新生命”为改造理念，如今也是吴淞口滨江观光景观区。

It is an international creative park gathering such fashionable elements as movie and television media, online games and animation production. According to the idea of "old buildings, old factories, new industries and new life", it has been transformed into the Wusongkou Riverside Sightseeing Area.

18

廿七　周五

上海国际展览中心

Intex Shanghai Co., Ltd.

长宁区兴义路 77 号

77 Xingyi Road, Changning District

全国首家获得 ISO9001 认证的国际性展览馆。建成于 1992 年，位于上海虹桥经济技术开发区，以国际性、贸易类展览会为主。其中乐器展和花卉展影响尤大。

Built in 1992 and located in Shanghai Hongqiao Economic and Technological Development Zone, it is the first international exhibition hall receiving ISO9001 certification in China, focusing on international and trade exhibitions. Musical instruments exhibition and flower shows held here are the most influential in China.

AUG. 19. 2017 SATURDAY

2017.8

农历丁酉年闰六月

19

廿八 周六

中国太平洋保险总部

HQ of China Pacific Insurance (Group) Co., Ltd (CPIC)

浦东新区银城中路 190 号交银金融大厦南楼
the South Building, Bocom Financial Tower,
190 Middle Yincheng Road, Pudong New Area

全国性大型保险公司，1991 年 5 月 13 日成立，总部设在陆家嘴金融城，2007 年在上交所上市。双塔楼 H 型造型，构思独特、设计巧妙，通过拱廊与相邻的建筑相连。

It is a typical nationwide insurance enterprise established on May 13,1991 with its headquarters located at the Lujiazui Financial City, and go public on the year 2007 in Shanghai Stock Exchange. The CPIC's office station is in a uniquely and creatively designed twin towers look like the character “H”, interconnected mutually with a high altitude arcade.

20

廿九　周日

上海书城
Shanghai Book Mall

黄浦区福州路 465 号
465 Fuzhou Road, Huangpu District

上海第一家超大型零售书店、上海重要文化活动中心之一，位于著名的文化街福州路，地标建筑。建成开业于 1998 年。楼高 27 层，其中 1–7 层用于图书零售。分设在各个层面有咖啡屋、面包房、阳光吧、纸艺吧和读者俱乐部。

Located at the famous cultural street —Fuzhou Road, Shanghai Book Mall is the first large retail bookstore in Shanghai and one of the important cultural activity centers. Founded and opened in 1998, it has become a landmark building with 27 floors, among which 1F-7F are dedicated to book retail. There are also cafes, bakeries, sunny bars, paper art barsand readers' clubson different floors.

AUG. 21. 2017 MONDAY *2017.8* 农历丁酉年闰六月

21

三十 周一

罗别根花园
Rubicon Garden

长宁区虹桥路 2310 号
2310 Hongqiao Road, Changning District

经典的英式尖顶花园别墅，上海最早的外国冒险家沙逊的私人别墅。因靠近旧时的罗别根路（今哈密路），故又被称为“罗别根花园”。市级文物保护单位。

The classic English-style steeple villa was the private villa of Shanghai's first foreign adventurer, Sassoon. This building is also known as the “Rubicon Garden” as it is near Rubicon Road (now Hami Road). It is a heritage site under municipal protection.

22

初一　周二

护珠塔
Huzhu Pagoda

松江区天马乡天马山
Tianma Mountain, Tianma Town, Songjiang District

古塔目前倾斜度已超过比萨斜塔。建于北宋元丰三年（1079），砖木结构，七层八面，高 18.82 米。相传塔里藏有舍利珠，夜间闪耀光芒，故得名。市级文物保护单位。

The ancient pagoda has currently tilted by larger degrees than the Pisa Tower. Built in 1079, it is an 18.82-meter brick-wooden structure with seven stories and eight facets. Legend has it that Buddhist relics are kept somewhere in the pagoda, giving out light at night. It is a heritage site under municipal protection.

AUG. 23. 2017 WEDNESDAY 2017.8 农历丁酉年七月

23

初二 周三

处暑

南翔寺砖塔

Brick Pagoda of Nanxiang Temple

嘉定区南翔镇
Nanxiang Town, Jiading District

上海现存年代最久远的古塔，建于梁天监年间的南翔寺的仅存遗物，是全国仅存的一对年代最悠久的仿木结构楼阁式砖塔，具有极高的文物和艺术价值。市级文物保护单位。

As the oldest ancient tower existing in Shanghai and the only remaining relics of Nangxiang Temple built in the Tianjian Period of Liang Dynasty during the Five Dynasties and Ten Kingdoms Period, the pagoda has a very high cultural and artistic value. It is a municipality protected historic and cultural site.

24

初三 周四

商船会馆

Merchant Shipping Hall

黄浦区中山南路 328 号
328 South Zhongshan Road, Huangpu District

始建于清康熙五十四年 (1715)，是上海商船运输业集资成立的第一个同乡同业公会所在地，内有双合式大殿、戏台、看戏厢房、集会议事大厅、神龛。市级文物保护单位。

Built in the 54th year of the reign of Emperor Kangxi in the Qing Dynasty (1715), the Merchant Shipping Hall is the location of the first guild funded and established by Shanghai merchant shipping industry. It is a municipality protected historic and cultural site.

25

初四　周五

上海国际舞蹈中心
Shanghai International Dance Center

长宁区虹桥路 1650 号
No. 1650, Hongqiao Road, Changning District

全国乃至亚洲第一个专业性舞蹈中心。总建筑面积 8.5 万平方米，聚集了上海专业舞蹈的“两团两校”4 家单位，连同两个剧院和 48 个排练厅，集舞蹈专业教育、创作与演出为一体。

On a par with the Centre National de la Danse (France), the Laban Dance Center (Britain) and the John F. Kennedy Center for the Performing Arts (U.S.), it is the first professional dance center in Asia. With an open setup, there is no fence around the buildings and thus they're directly connected with the Yanhong Green Land. It is regarded as a new cultural landmark of Shanghai that features both culture and green space.

26

初五　周六

上海大剧院

Shanghai Grand Theatre

黄浦区黄陂北路 286 号
286 North Huangpi Roadi, Huangpu District

1998 年 8 月 27 日开业

上海的标志性文化设施。位于市中心、毗邻市政府大厦，建筑风格独特，造型优美。1998 年开业，成为上海重要的中外文化交流窗口和艺术沟通的桥梁。

It is a landmark cultural facility of Shanghai, located at the center of Shanghai and adjacent to the Municipal Government. Opened in 1998, the theatre with unique architectural style and beautiful modeling has become an increasingly important window for cultural exchange between China and foreign countries and also a bridge of art communication in Shanghai.

AUG. 27. 2017 SUNDAY

2017.8

农历丁酉年七月

27

初六　周日

大悦城屋顶摩天轮

Ferris Wheel on the Rooftop of Joy City

静安区西藏北路 166 号大悦城屋顶
No. 166, Joy City, North Xizang Road, Jing' an District

浪漫七夕，在此相会

国内首个悬臂式屋顶摩天轮，直径 56 米，距离地面 98 米，拥有 30 个极具时尚感的白色轿舱。360° 动感浪漫搭乘体验，搭配下午茶及夜色大餐，使其荣膺上海新地标之称。

It is the first cantilever rooftop ferris wheel in China with 30 white fashionable cabins, 56 m in diameter and 98 m above the ground. The 360-degree dynamic and romantic experience, together with the afternoon tea and gorgeous night views make it the new landmark of Shanghai.

28

初七　周一

七夕节

K11 购物艺术中心
K11 Art Mall

黄浦区淮海中路 300 号
300 Middle Huaihai Road, Huangpu District

坐落于淮海路黄金地带，秉承“艺术·人文·自然”相融合的品牌理念，在艺术欣赏、人文体验、自然绿化以及购物消费的创意互动中，为大众带来全新的体验。

Located at the prime commercial area of Huaihai Road, it adheres to the brand concept of integrating “art, humanity and nature” and brings the unprecedented sensory experience for the people in the art appreciation, human experience, natural landscaping and creative interaction of shopping.

29

初八　周二

张闻天故居
Zhang Wentian's Former Residence

浦东新区机场镇闻居路 50 号
50 Wenju Road, Jichang Town, Pudong New Area

1900 年 8 月 30 日张闻天在此诞生

中共早期领导人之一张闻天诞生地和青少年时期生活场所。一幢具有浦东农村传统风格的一正两厢的瓦房。全国重点文物保护单位。

It is the place where Zhang Wentian, one of the earliest leaders of the Communist Party of China, was born and bred. It is a tile-roofed house with a central room and two wing rooms, striking the right note of a traditional rural house in the Pudong area. It is an important heritage site under state protection.

AUG. 30. 2017 WEDNESDAY　2017.8　农历丁酉年七月

30

初九　周三

杜莎夫人蜡像馆
Madame Tussaud's

黄浦区南京西路 2–68 号新世界商厦 10 楼
10/F, New World Building, 2–68 West Nanjing Road, Huangpu District

全球第6座杜莎夫人蜡像馆。分为“在幕后”、“上海魅力”、“历史名人和国家领袖”、“电影”、“音乐”、“运动”和“速度”七个主题展区。

As the sixth place of Madame Tussauds in the world, it falls into seven theme exhibition areas, namely “Behind the scenes”, “Shanghai Charm”, “Historical figures and national leaders”, “Movie”, “Music”, “Sports” and “Speed”.

31

初十　周四

影像·中国
上海地标
2017

玖
September
月

汇龙潭

Huilong Pond

嘉定区嘉定镇塔城路 299 号
No. 299, Tacheng Road, Jiading Town, Jiading District

建于明代万历年间，因自北向南有五条河流汇集而成，应奎山坐落潭中，宛如“五龙抢珠”而得名。园内南部是自然山水风景，北部为夕照亭等人文景点。

Built in the period reigned by the Wanli Emperor of the Ming Dynasty, it is one of the five classical gardens in Shanghai. From the north to the south, five rivers join here with Mount Yingkui standing in the pond, just like “five dragons grabbing a ball” and hence the name. The south of the garden is natural landscape while the north of it sees cultural attractions like Sunset Pavilion.

1

十一　周五

月星环球港

Yuexing Global Harbor

普陀区中山北路 3222 号
3222 North Zhongshan Road, Putuo District

高档生活品质的大型商业综合体，首次全面提出“商、旅、文”三大中心功能概念，提供“不用出国门的欧洲商旅体验”。

It is a large commercial complex which demonstrates the civilizations of the East and the West and the top quality of life. It comprehensively puts forward the function concept of three centers “business, travel and culture” for the first time, and functions as a wind vane to lead the latest concept of fashion and cultural life in city.

SEP. 2. 2017 SATURDAY

2017.9

农历丁酉年七月

2

十二　周六

浦东国际机场
Pudong International Airport

浦东新区启航路 300 号
300 Qihang Road, Pudong New Area

1999 年 9 月第一航站楼启用

上海两大国际机场之一，与北京首都国际机场、香港国际机场并称中国三大国际机场。1999 年建成通航。主楼建筑外形犹如展翅飞翔的海鸥，具有强烈的时代感和象征意义。

As one of the two major international airports of Shanghai, Shanghai Pudong International Airport is known as one of China's three major international airports, together with Beijing Capital International Airport and Hong Kong International Airport. It was put into service in 1999.

SEP. 3. 2017 SUNDAY 2017.9 农历丁酉年七月

3

十三　周日

抗战胜利纪念日

李塔

Li Pagoda

松江区石湖荡镇李塔汇
Litahui, Shihudang Town, Songjiang District

又称“礼塔”，是一座砖木结构的七级方塔，据清代《李塔延寿寺院记》，始建于唐朝初期。高约 33 米，各层壶门外的壁上嵌有 200 尊形态各异的佛雕。市级文物保护单位。

Also known as Ceremony Pagoda, Li Pagoda is a seven-storied square pagoda of brick-wood structure. It is about 33 meters high with 200 Buddhist carvings of different shapes embedded in the walls outside the Humen (a door form in Buddhist architecture). It is a municipality protected historic and cultural site.

SEP. 4. 2017 MONDAY　2017.9　农历丁酉年七月

4

十四　周一

永安公司（华联商厦）

Wing On Company (Hualian Department Store)

黄浦区南京东路 627 号
627 East Nanjing Road, Huangpu District

1918 年 9 月 5 日开业

旧上海百货四大公司之一，也是中国近代最大的百货公司，中华商业老字号，至今仍为上海高档百货商店。旧时是南京路上仅次于国际饭店的第二高楼。市级文物保护单位。

As one of the four major department stores in Shanghai before 1949, Wing On Company is also the largest department store in modern China. As a China Time-honored Brand, it is still an upscale department store in Shanghai now. It is a historical and cultural site protected at the municipal level now.

5

十五 周二

中元节

碧云国际创意园区
Biyun International Creative Park

浦东新区金桥开发区
Jinqiao Development Zone, Pudong New Area

依托国家级重点开发区金桥开发区众多跨国通信、IT 企业，结合浦东外向型、多功能、国际化现状和需求打造的多元、开放、创新的新型国际 CBD，有“小联合国”的美称。

It is a diversified, open, and innovative new-type international CBD built in combination with the export-oriented, multi-functional and internationalized status and needs of Pudong and depending on a number of transnational telecommunication and IT enterprises in Jinqiao Development Zone - one of national key development zones. It is reputed as the “mini-type United Nations”.

6

十六　周三

曲水园
Qushui Park

青浦区城厢公园路 650 号
650 Chengxiang Park Road, Qingpu District

2007 年 9 月修缮开放

初建于清乾隆十年（1745），建筑以青瓦、白墙、青砖构成，小巧玲珑、典雅古朴，因园在大盈浦旁，名取“曲水流觞”之意。上海五大古典园林之一，四星级公园。

Built in 1745 under the reign of the Emperor Qianlong in Qing Dynasty, Qushui Park, with grey tiles, white walls and grey bricks, is famous for its exquisite and elegant style. And the park was named after the bending brooks as it was close to Daying Riverside. It is one of the five classical gardens in Shanghai and a four-star park.

SEP. 7. 2017 THURSDAY　　2017.9　　农历丁酉年七月

7

十七　周四

白露

孔公馆

Kung Mansion

虹口区多伦路 250 号
250 Duolun Road, Hongkou District

建于 1924 年，浓厚伊斯兰情调的西班牙风格砖木结构二层住宅。曾为孔祥熙沪上四处豪居之一，俗称“孔公馆”。市级文物保护单位。

Built in 1924, this Spanish-style two-story brick house with a strong Islamic flavor was once one of Kung Hsiang-hsi's four Luxury residences in Shanghai known as the "Kung Mansion". It is a heritage site under municipal protection.

SEP. 8. 2017 FRIDAY

2017.9

农历丁酉年七月

8

十八　周五

裕华新村

Yuhua New Residential Quarter

静安区富民路 182 弄
Lane 182 Fumin Road, Jing'an District

始建于 1941 年，共 36 幢房屋，后期新式里弄住宅，旧上海里弄风情绝佳处之一，皆三层砖木结构，坐北朝南，带小花园。李鸿章部分后裔仍住于此。市级文物保护单位。

Built in 1941 and composed of 36 houses, Yuhua New Residential Quarter is a late modern residential neighborhood, a great place to experience the flavor of old Shanghai neighborhood. It is a heritage site under municipal protection.

SEP. 9. 2017 SATURDAY

2017.9

农历丁酉年七月

9

十九　周六

华东师范大学
East China Normal University

普陀区中山北路 3663 号
3663 North Zhongshan Road, Putuo District

前身是 1924 年成立的大夏大学，1951 年在其原址上创办的综合性研究型大学，涵盖文史哲、经济、法学、教育学、心理学、理工、管理学、医学、艺术学 11 个学科门类。

Founded in 1951, East China Normal University is a comprehensive research-oriented university jointly established by the Ministry of Education and Shanghai Municipal government. It was listed among Project 211 institutions in 1996 and was listed among Project 985 institutions in 2006.

SEP. 10. 2017 SUNDAY　2017.9　农历丁酉年七月

10

二十　周日

教师节

上海电影博物馆

Shanghai Film Museum

徐汇区漕溪北路 595 号
595 North Caoxi Road, Xuhui District

国内规模最大的电影博物馆，原为市级文物保护单位上影厂大院，馆内黄楼原为天主教修女道场圣衣院。博物馆有四大主题展区、一座多功能厅及一座艺术影厅等。

It is China's largest film museum, the former site of Shanghai Film Studios under municipal protection as part of Shanghai's cultural heritage. The yellow building in it used to be the Carmelite Convent of Catholic nuns. There are four areas named "Honorable Hall", "Film Studio", "Film History" and "Film Memory" in the Museum.

SEP. 11. 2017 MONDAY

2017.9

农历丁酉年七月

11

廿一　周一

尚贤坊

Shangxian Fang

黄浦区淮海中路 358 弄
Lane 358 Middle Huaihai Road, Huangpu District

代表性的上海里弄石库门建筑，取名缘于美国传教士李佳白所开设的“尚贤堂”。旧时住户以教师、作家居多，据说郁达夫与王映霞的爱情诞生于此。市级文物保护单位。

It is a typical Shanghai Shikumen neighborhood building, and the reported birthplace of the love between the famous writer Yu Dafu and Wang Yingxia. It is a heritage site under municipal protection.

12

廿二　周二

马戏城

Circus World

静安区共和新路 2266 号
2266 Gonghexin Road, Jing'an District

1999 年 9 月开业

静安区的文化、体育、娱乐中心，有“中国马戏第一城”的美誉，以其主体建筑杂技场造型独特的金色穹型屋顶，成为上海国际文化都市的一个标志性建筑。

Reputed as “China's No. 1 Circus World”, it is the center of culture, sports and entertainment of Jing'an District. With unique architectural shape of a golden dome-like roof, Shanghai Circus World has become a landmark in the international cultural metropolis Shanghai.

SEP. 13. 2017 WEDNESDAY　　*2017.9*　　农历丁酉年七月

13

廿三　周三

盛宣怀住宅（日本领事馆）

The Residence of Sheng Xuanhuai (the Consulate General of Japan)

徐汇区淮海中路 1517 号
1517 Middle Huaihai Road, Xuhui District

1912 年秋盛宣怀定居于此

建于 1900 年，因曾为清代洋务派主要人物盛宣怀购得，遂称为盛宣怀住宅。新古典主义风格花园洋房，三层砖木结构。建国后为日本国驻上海领事馆。市级文物保护单位。

Built in 1900, it is called the residence of Sheng Xuanhuai as it was ever purchased by Sheng Xuanhuai, a major influential westernizationist in the Qing Dynasty. After Chinese and Japan resumed diplomatic relations, the Consulate General of Japan in Shanghai was once located here. It is now a historical and cultural site protected at the municipal level.

SEP. 14. 2017 THURSDAY

2017.9

农历丁酉年七月

14

廿四　周四

丰子恺旧居

The Former Residence of Feng Zikai

黄浦区陕西南路 39 弄 93 号
93 Lane 39, South Shaanxi Road, Luwan District

1975 年 9 月 15 日丰子恺在此逝世

我国现代著名画家、散文家、美术教育家、音乐教育家、漫画家、书法家和翻译家丰子恺从 1954 年到逝世时一直在此居住。寓所属西班牙联列式结构建筑。现内辟陈列室。

It was the residence of Feng Zikai, a modern famous painter, proser, art educationist, music educator, cartoonist, calligrapher and translator of China, from 1954 to his death in Shanghai. It is a Spanish column-style building with a showroom inside.

15

廿五　周五

《新青年》编辑部旧址（陈独秀旧居）

Former Site of the Newsroom of *New Youth* (Former Residence of Chen Duxiu)

黄浦区南昌路 100 弄 2 号
2 Lane 100, Nanchang Road, Huangpu District

1915 年 9 月 15 日《新青年》创刊

1915 年 9 月 15 日创刊、陈独秀主编的新文化运动的核心刊物、中共早期机关刊物《新青年》编辑部所在地。市级文物保护单位。

Started on September 15, 1915, *New Youth* was a core journal for the New Culture Movement and an early journal of CPC under the general editorship of Chen Duxiu. This is where the newsroom of *New Youth* was located. It is a heritage site under municipal protection.

SEP. 16. 2017 SATURDAY

2017.9

农历丁酉年七月

16

廿六　周六

董家渡天主堂

Dongjiadu Church

黄浦区董家渡路 175 号
175 Dongjiadu Road, Huangpu District

上海近现代第一座，也是现存最完整、最古老的天主教堂，仿照罗马耶稣会总会的圣依纳爵大堂建造，外形为巴洛克式风格，室内为文艺复兴时代风格。市级文物保护单位。

It was the first cathedral in Modern Shanghai, and also the most complete and oldest Catholic Church in Shanghai. It is a heritage site under municipal protection.

SEP. 17. 2017 SUNDAY

2017.9

农历丁酉年七月

17

廿七　周日

中共淞浦特委办公地点旧址

Former Office Site of Songpu Special Committee of CPC

静安区山海关路 387 弄 5 号
5 Lane 387, Shanhaiguan Road, Jing'an District

1928 年 9 月淞浦特委成立

中共淞浦特委办公地点旧址是 1928 年中共江苏省委淞浦特委启用的办公所在地。市级文物保护单位。

It is the location of former office used by the Songpu Special Committee of CPC in Jiangsu Province in 1928. It is now a municipality protected historic and cultural site.

18

廿八　周一

上海植物园

Shanghai Botanical Garden

徐汇区龙吴路 1111 号
1111 Longwu Road, Xuhui District

每年 9 月底到 10 月秋季花展

一个以植物引种驯化和展示、园艺研究及科普教育为主的综合性植物园。每年举办各类花展及科普活动。国家 4A 景区。

It's a comprehensive botanical garden that primarily focuses on plant domestication and exhibition, horticultural research, and science promotion and education. Many flower shows and science promotion activities are held every year in the garden. It is a 4A-rated national tourist attraction.

19

廿九　周二

2577 创意大院
2577 Creative Garden

徐汇区龙华路 2577 号
2577 Longhua Road, Xuhui District

1865 年 9 月 20 日江南枪炮局创办

最早为李鸿章创办的江南枪炮局，中国现代工业设计的发源地。有反映不同时期的历史风貌建筑几十处，现为上海市新传媒创意产业园区的一个新地标。

Formerly known as the Jiangnan Firearms Factory established by Li Hung-chang, it was the cradle of China's modern industrial design. It features dozens of historical buildings at different times. Now it is a new landmark of new media creative industry of Shanghai.

SEP. 20. 2017 WEDNESDAY　*2017.9*　农历丁酉年八月

20

初一　周三

和平公园

Peace Park

虹口区大连路 1131 号
1131 Dalian Road, Hongkou District

9 月 21 日世界和平日

以中国自然山水园林风格为特色的综合性公园，共分风景游览区、动物观赏区、儿童娱乐区三大景区。园址曾为旅沪犹太人避难所、日军弹药库。为教育后人热爱和平而得名。

Peace Park is a comprehensive park featured with the style of China's natural landscape gardens. It is divided into three scenic areas: landscape area, animal viewing area and children recreation area. It was the refuge of Jews who traveled to Shanghai and the ammunition depot of the Japanese forces, and got its name for educating the offspring to love peace.

21

初二　周四

桂林公园

Guilin Park

徐汇区桂林路 128 号
128 Guilin Road, Xuhui District

始建于 1929 年，原系旧上海著名青帮头目黄金荣私人别墅，又名黄家花园。建国后辟为公园，因园内遍植桂花树，故得名。造园艺术以经典江南传统著称。

Completed in 1929, it was the private villa of Huang Jinrong, a leader of the Green Gang (a Chinese secret society and criminal organization, which was prominent in criminal and political activity in Shanghai during the early 20th century), also known as Huang's Garden. It was rebuilt into a park after the founding of the People's Republic of China. It got its name for Osmanthus Fragrans across the park. The garden art is famous for the traditions of the regions south of the Yangtze River.

22

初三　周五

中国民族乐器博物馆

Chinese Traditional Musical Instruments Museum

闵行区七莘路 1 号
No.1 Qixin Road, Minhang District

9 月 23 日中国民族音乐节

国内展品最为丰富、规模最大、最具特色的民族乐器博物馆。由上海民族乐器一厂创意筹建，1986 年正式开馆。展品有四大系列，一百余品种，三百多件实物。

It is China's largest museum of Chinese traditional musical instruments, with the most abundant and featured exhibits. It was built out of the creativity of Shanghai NO.1 National Musical Instruments Factory and opened officially in 1986. The museum has a collection of four series, more than 300 pieces of over 100 varieties.

23

初四　周六

秋分

思南公馆

Sinan Mansions

黄浦区复兴中路 523 号
523 Middle Fuxing Road, Huangpu District

市中心唯一一个以成片花园洋房的保留、保护为宗旨、坐拥 51 栋老花园洋房的优秀历史建筑保护改造区，包括思南公馆酒店、特色名店商业区、公寓和企业公馆等。

It is the only protection and renovation area of excellent historical architecture with 51 old foreign-style garden houses and for the purpose of preservation and protection of the large expanse of foreign-style garden houses, comprising Hotel Massenet at Sinan Mansions, business area of featured famous stores, apartments and Cotels.

SEP. 24. 2017 SUNDAY

2017.9

农历丁酉年八月

24

初五　周日

修道院公寓（湖南街道办事处）

Convent Apartment (Hunan Sub-district Office)

徐汇区复兴西路 62 号
62 West Fuxing Road, Xuhui District

原为旧上海英商密丰绒线厂厂主的住宅，建筑的外观和室内装修均为典型西班牙风格，因内部空间组合富有层次和变化而闻名，保存较好。市级文物保护单位。

Originally being the residence of the owner of British Mifeng Wool Factory, Convent Apartment is known as an atypical Spanish-style structure. It is a heritage site under municipal protection.

25

初六 周一

兴国宾馆 1 号楼

Building 1 of Xing Guo Hotel

长宁区兴国路 72 号
72 Xingguo Road, Changning District

建于 1935 年，英国帕拉第奥式古典主义建筑，原系太古洋行大班 Swire 的住宅，巨型紫铜板屋顶已氧化成绿色，俗称“铜房子”。建国后为国宾馆。市级文物保护单位。

Built in 1935, this two-story brick-concrete building is a classical British architecture of Palladian style. It is a heritage site under municipal protection.

SEP. 26. 2017 TUESDAY　　*2017.9*　　农历丁酉年八月

26

初七　周二

召稼楼古镇

Zhaojialou Ancient Town

闵行区浦江镇革新村内
in Gexin Village, Pujiang Town, Minhang District

园林景观剧《梦回召稼楼》2013 年 9 月 27 日首演

古镇横跨元明清三个朝代，面积达 150 亩之广，散落着不少清代建筑，目前规模较大、保存较完整的有“礼耕堂”、“梅园”等。召楼大曲、召楼羊肉、召楼拆蹄为古镇三宝。

The ancient town has lived through Yuan, Ming and Qing Dynasties and covers an area of 150 mu. There are many scattered buildings of the Qing Dynasty, among which “Ligeng Hall” and “Plum Garden”, etc. are large in scale and well preserved. Daqu, a traditional music of Han nationality, mutton and split hoofs are acclaimed as three treasures of the ancient town.

SEP. 27. 2017 WEDNESDAY *2017.9* 农历丁酉年八月

27

初八 周三

宝山孔庙大成殿

Dacheng Hall of Confucian Temple in Baoshan District

宝山区友谊路 1 号临江公园内
Inside Linjiang Park, No. 1 Youyi Road, Baoshan District

公元前 551 年 9 月 28 日孔子诞辰

亦称“圣人殿”，始建于清乾隆十二年（1747），是上海现存四大孔庙之一的宝山文庙的主要建筑之一。殿内雕龙贴金的巨龛中供着孔子的塑像。市级文物保护单位。

Also known as the “Saint Temple”, it is one of the main buildings of Baoshan Temple of Literature, one of the four extant Confucian temples in Shanghai. It is now a municipality protected historic and cultural site.

28

初九　周四

中国（上海）自由贸易试验区

China (Shanghai) Pilot Free Trade Zone

浦东新区
in Pudong New Area

2013 年 9 月 29 日挂牌成立

中国政府 2013 年起设在上海的区域性自由贸易园区。面积 28.78 平方公里，涵盖外高桥保税区、洋山保税港区、浦东机场综合保税区、金桥出口加工区等七个区域。

It is a regional free trade zone established by the Chinese government in Shanghai in 2013, covering an area of 28.78 square kilometers. This Zone consists of seven areas, including Waigaoqiao Bonded Zone, Yangshan Free Trade Port Area, Pudong Airport Free Trade Zone and Jinqiao Export Processing Zone.

29

初十　周五

张爱玲故居

The Former Residence of Eileen Zhang

静安区常德路 999 号
999 Changde Road, Jing'an District

1920 年 9 月 30 日张爱玲出生日

常德公寓，是中国现代文学史上重要作家、才女张爱玲的故居，一幢建于 20 世纪 30 年代初的法式公寓建筑。张爱玲曾在这幢楼的 601 室生活了 5 年。

Changde Apartment, a French-style apartment built in the 1930s, is the former residence of Eileen Zhang, an important writer and talented woman in history of Chinese contemporary literature. She had been living in Room 601 of this building for 5 years.

30

十一　周六

影像·中国
上海地标
2017
Hapag-Lloyd

拾
October
月

人民广场
People's Square

黄浦区
in Huangpu District

上海融文化、绿化、美化为一体的政治、经济、文化、旅游中心和交通枢纽，上海市最为重要的地标之一，由开放式广场、人民公园以及周边景观组成，总面积达 14 万平方米。

As the most significant landmark of Shanghai and a combination of culturalization, verdurization and beautification turnout, the square is a multiple area functioning as Shanghai's political, economic, cultural center and the urban transportation hub which consists of the open-air square, the People's Park and others public facilities nearby. The total area of the People's Square amounts to more than 140 thousand square meters.

OCT. 1. 2017 SUNDAY

2017.10

农历丁酉年八月

1

十二　周日

国庆节

黄炎培故居

Former Residence of Huang Yanpei

浦东新区川沙镇新川路 218 号
218 Xinchuan Road, Chuansha Town, Pudong New Area

1878 年 10 月 1 日黄炎培在此出生

近现代著名的爱国主义教育家、政治家、社会活动家黄炎培的诞生、成长地。古色古香的二层砖木结构楼房，粉墙黑瓦，雕梁画栋。内设有陈列室。市级文物保护单位。

Also known as the "Neishidi Residence" and "Courtyard of the Shen Family", the place is where Huang Yanpei was born and grew up. There is a Showroom of Huang Yanpei's life. It is now a municipality protected historic and cultural site.

2

十三 周一

《布尔什维克》编辑部旧址

Former Site of the Newsroom of Bolshevik

长宁区愚园路 1376 弄 34 号
34 Lane 1376, Yuyuan Road, Changning District

1927 年 10 月创刊

建党初期中共中央宣传部机关及党中央机关刊物《布尔什维克》编辑部所在地，地处上海著名红色弄堂“亨昌里”。市级文物保护单位。

It is where the newsroom of Bolshevik, the journal for organs of the Publicity Department of Central CPC on its inception and is located in “Hengchang Lane” – the well-known red lane in Shanghai. It is a heritage site under municipal protection.

3

十四　周二

上海动物园
Shanghai Zoo

长宁区虹桥路 2381 号
2381 Hongqiao Road, Changning District

10 月 4 日世界动物日

中国第二大城市动物园、全国十佳动物园，也是上海市区最佳的生态园林之一。园内珍稀野生动物种类繁多，还有中国大陆动物园中第一座科学教育馆。国家 4A 景区。

It is the second largest urban zoo in China, one of the top ten zoos in China, and one of the best ecological gardens in downtown Shanghai. The zoo boasts many species of rare wild animals and the first science education center among all the zoos of Mainland China. It is a 4A-rated national tourist attraction.

OCT. 4. 2017 WEDNESDAY 2017.10 农历丁酉年八月

4

十五 周三

中秋节

美琪大戏院（美琪影剧院）

Majestic Theatre

静安区江宁路 66 号
66 Jiangning Road, Jing'an District

1941 年 10 月开业

建于 1941 年，名字取意“美轮美奂，琪玉无瑕”，曾被誉为“亚洲第一大戏院”，是旧上海各种大型演出剧场。解放初一度成为重要政治活动集会场所。市级文物保护单位。

Built in 1941, Majestic Theatre was hailed as “Asia’s largest theater” at home and abroad, the theater for various large-scale performances in Shanghai before 1949, and was an important meeting place for political activities after the Liberation War. It is a heritage site under municipal protection.

5

十六　周四

西侨青年会大楼（体育大厦）
Former Foreign YMCA Building (Sports Building)

黄浦区南京西路 150 号
150 West Nanjing Road, Huangpu District

1929 年 10 月奠基

上世纪 20 年代美国人菲奇和洛克菲勒为旅沪西方青年建造的文娱馆所。采用美国工艺美术派风格，古典精致。建国后为上海市体育俱乐部、市体委所在地。市级文物保护单位。

This classical and exquisite building of arts and crafts style of the United States was built by Americans, Fitch and Rockefeller, for the Western youth in Shanghai for culture and recreation purpose in the 1920s. It is a heritage site under municipal protection.

OCT. 6. 2017 FRIDAY

2017.10

农历丁酉年八月

6

十七　周五

车墩影视基地

Film Shooting Base

松江区车墩镇北松公路 4915 号
4915 Beisong Road, Chedun Town, Songjiang District

10 月上海国际电影节

又名上海影视乐园，有旧上海的市井风情，有拍电影的幕后秘密，为人们重睹旧上海风情开辟了全新的途径。关于上海的影视剧大多取景于此，如《色·戒》、《新上海滩》等。

Also known as Shanghai Film Park, it shows local customs of Old Shanghai and secrets for film shooting, thus providing a new way for people to feel the charm of old Shanghai. Movies and teleplays about Shanghai, such as Lust, Caution and Shanghai Bund are mostly set here.

OCT. 7. 2017 SATURDAY

2017.10

农历丁酉年八月

7

十八　周六

古银杏树公园

Old Gingko Park

嘉定区安亭镇光明村
Guangming village, Anting Town, Jiading District

嘉定区政府为保护一棵树龄 1200 余年的上海银杏树“树王”而辟建的公园。主园路设有花架、木廊，配置湖石假山、汀步，古色古香的弹街路通向各景点。

The park was built by Jiading District Government to protect the 1,200-year old gingko king of Shanghai. There are pergolas and wooden corridors along the main road with rockeries and stepping stones over water. The antique cobblestone pavements lead to the scenic sites.

OCT. 8. 2017 SUNDAY　　2017.10　　农历丁酉年八月

8

十九　周日

寒露

上海邮政总局

General Post Office Building, Shanghai

虹口区北苏州路 276 号
276 North Suzhou Road, Hongkou District

10 月 9 日世界邮政日

仍在使用的建筑最早、规模最大的邮政标志性建筑，见证我国邮政事业近现代化过程。整体建筑风格为 19 世纪到 20 世纪初流行欧美的折衷主义。全国重点文物保护单位。

It is the earliest and largest iconic postal building which is still in use, and has witnessed the modernization process of the postal undertaking of China. The general style of the building is a reflection of eclecticism which was popular in Europe and America from the 19th century to the early 20th century. It is an important heritage site under state protection.

9

二十 周一

东方绿舟——上海市青少年校外活动营地

Oriental Land—Shanghai Teenagers Extra-curricular Activities Campsite

青浦区沪青平公路 6888 号
6888 Huqingping Highway, Qingpu District

集拓展培训、青少年实践、团队活动以及休闲旅游于一体的大型主题公园。植被苍翠、风光旖旎，有拓展训练、水上运动、军事体验等 30 余种活动。内有航母模型。国家 4A 景区。

It is the only large theme park that integrates development training, teenager practice, group activities and leisure & tourism. In addition to lush vegetation and charming scenery, it provides more than 30 kinds of activities, including development trainings, water sports and military experience. It is a 4A-rated national tourist attraction.

OCT. 10. 2017 TUESDAY

2017.10

农历丁酉年八月

10

廿一　周二

旗忠森林网球中心

Qizhong Forest Sports City Arena

闵行区马桥镇元江路 5500 号
5500 Yuanjiang Road, Maqiao Town, Minhang District

每年 10 月中旬上海国际网球大师赛在此举行

世界一流水准的多功能比赛场馆，可举办各种世界最高级别比赛。场馆建筑获中国土木工程“詹天佑奖”，顶棚开启方式仿佛白玉兰的开花过程，为世界首创。

It is a multi-purpose arena of the world's first-class standard and enables to hold various matches of the world's highest levels. The arena building was granted the "Zhan Tianyou Awards" for Chinese civil engineering. The openable ceiling resembles a blooming michelia alba when it's being opened, which is the first of its kind in the world.

11

廿二 周三

外滩观光隧道

Bund Sightseeing Tunnel

外滩中山东一路 300 号（浦西），浦东新区滨江大道 2789 号（浦东）

300 East Zhongshan Road No.1, the Bund (in Puxi), 2789 Riverside Promenade, Pudong New Area (in Pudong)

2000 年 10 月开通

中国首条越江行人隧道，位于南京东路外滩和东方明珠广播电视塔之间黄浦江底，全长 646.70 米，是融交通与旅游功能为一体的标志性景观工程，隧道建筑史上的创举。

The Bund Sightseeing Tunnel is Shanghai's first pedestrian tunnel across the Huangpu River and also China's first pedestrian tunnel across the river. Located between the Bund of Nanjing East Road and the Oriental Pearl Radio & TV Tower, the tunnel with a total length of 646.70 meters is a landmark landscape with integrated functions of traffic and tourism, and honored as a pioneering work in the history of tunnel construction.

12

廿三　周四

新江湾城 SMP 滑板公园

SMP Skatepark

杨浦区淞沪路 2100 号
2100 Songhu Road, Yangpu District

2005 年 10 月开放

全球最大的极限运动主题公园。可进行直排轮、滑板、BMX 小轮车、摩托车等各类极限运动项目，场地分“街区”、“碗槽”、“U 型台”及比赛区域等多层次设计。

SMP Skatepark is the world's largest X-game theme park. It features various X-game sports projects such as in-line skating, skate board, BMX and motorcycle, and multi-level design of fields, such as “street section”, “skate bowls”, “U-shaped platform” and competition area.

13

廿四 周五

嘉定州桥

Jiading Zhou Bridge

嘉定镇街道

Sub-district of Jiading Town

2008 年 10 月嘉定古镇被认定为“中国历史文化名镇”

也称登龙桥，是一条始建于南宋淳祐五年（1245）的单孔石拱桥，人称“嘉定之根”。在千步之内汇集了宋、元、明、清历代古塔、旧庙、名园而为国内罕见。国家 4A 景区。

It is a single arch stone bridge first built in the fifth year of the Chunyou period of South Song Dynasty (A.D.1245), also called Denglong Bridge and the "Root of Jiading". In a walk of about one thousand steps around the attraction, one may see ancient pagodas, temples and gardens built in Song, Yuan, Ming and Qing Dynasties, which is rarely seen in China. It is a 4A-rated national tourist attraction.

14

廿五 周六

沉香阁

Chen Xiang Pavilion

黄浦区沉香阁路 29 号
29 Chen Xiang Pavilion Road, Huangpu District

1992 年 10 月 15 日沉香观音开光典礼

旧名慈云禅寺，初创于明代万历二十八年（1600），是上海市著名的佛教比丘尼道场，也是上海唯一供奉沉香观音的寺院。全国重点寺院和全国重点文物保护单位。

Formerly known as Ciyun Temple, it was first built in the 28th year of the Wanli period in the Ming Dynasty (A.D.1600). Now it is a famous Bhikkhuni convent in Shanghai and the only temple worshiping an eaglewood statue of Guanyin in Shanghai. It is one of the key national temples and one of the major cultural sites protected at the national level.

OCT. 15. 2017 SUNDAY

2017.10

农历丁酉年八月

15

廿六　周日

新康花园

Xinkang Garden Residence

徐汇区淮海中路 1273 号
1273 Middle Huaihai Road, Xuhui District

1949 年 9 月 10 日更名为新康花园

建于 1934 年，公寓式里弄的典型代表，为日后上海城市住宅区的整体面貌奠定了基础。外观为西班牙式，宅后有庭院，种植雪松。大批英国侨民曾在此居住。市级文物保护单位。

As a typical apartment-style neighborhood, Xinkang Garden Residence was built in 1934 and laid the foundation for the overall outlook of Shanghai's urban residential area for the times to come. It is a heritage site under municipal protection.

OCT. 16. 2017 MONDAY　*2017.10*　农历丁酉年八月

16

廿七　周一

巴金上海故居

The Former Residence of Ba Jin

徐汇区武康路 113 号
113 Wukang Road, Xuhui District

2005 年 10 月 17 日巴金逝世

现代著名作家、翻译家、社会活动家、无党派爱国民主人士巴金先生于 1955-1995 年间在上海生活居住的寓所，是一幢独立式花园洋房。

It is the residence of Mr. Ba Jin, a modern famous writer, translator, social activist and nonpartisan patriotic democratic personage of China in Shanghai during the period between 1955 and 1995, and also a holy land of literature in the heart of thousands of readers. It is an independent foreign garden-style house.

17

廿八　周二

陶行知纪念馆

Tao Xingzhi Memorial Hall

宝山区武威东路 76 号
76 East Wuwei Road, Baoshan District

1986 年 10 月 18 日陶行知诞辰日对外开放

现代著名教育家、思想家，伟大的民主主义战士，爱国者，中国人民救国会和民盟的主要领导人之一陶行知在上海的纪念馆。

It is the memorial hall of Tao Xingzhi, a modern well-known educator, ideologist, great democratic soldier, patriot and one of major leaders of Chinese National Salvation Association and China Democratic League, in Shanghai.

OCT. 18. 2017 WEDNESDAY 2017.10 农历丁酉年八月

18

廿九 周三

鲁迅纪念馆

Lu Xun Memorial Hall

虹口区甜爱路 200 号
200 Tian'ai Road, Hongkou District

1936 年 10 月 19 日鲁迅逝世

新中国成立后第一个建设开放的人物性纪念馆。以鲁迅故居、鲁迅墓、鲁迅纪念馆的生平陈列三位一体。馆舍是二层庭院式的江南民居风格的建筑。国家一级博物馆。

As the first character memorial museum built and opened after 1949, Shanghai Lu Xun Memorial Hall is composed of the former Residence of Lu Xun, Lu Xun tomb, and Lu Xun Memorial Hall. It is a Grade-One national museum.

OCT. 19. 2017 THURSDAY　　2017.10　　农历丁酉年八月

19

三十　周四

《中国青年》编辑部旧址

Former Site of the Newsroom of *China Youth*

黄浦区淡水路 66 弄 4 号
4 Lane 66, Danshui Road, Huangpu District

1923 年 10 月 20 日《中国青年》创刊

旧址是 1923 年中国社会主义青年团机关刊物、也是唯一一本延续至今的党办刊物《中国青年》的编辑部诞生地，是一幢坐北朝南、二层石库门住宅。市级文物保护单位。

This is the birthplace of the newsroom of *China Youth*, the official journal of the Socialist Youth League of China started in 1923 and the only CPC journal lasting to date. Being a two-story south-facing Shikumen residence, it is a heritage site under municipal protection.

20

初一　周五

国际会议中心

International Convention Center

浦东新区滨江大道 2727 号

2727 Riverside Promenade, Pudong New Area

2001 年 10 月 21 日 APEC 第九次领导人非正式会议在此举行

地处陆家嘴金融贸易中心，与外滩万国建筑群隔江相望，乳白色外墙托起两只巨大球体的建筑外观极具特征，总面积达 11 万平方米，以举办大型国际会议、商务论坛而蜚声海内外。

Facing the exotic building clusters in the Bund across the Huangpu River, Shanghai International Convention Center is located in the Lujiazui Financial District. The appearance of the Center is like two gigantic spheres being held up by milky white walls. It covers an area of 110,000 m2 and is well known home and abroadas a venue for large international conferences and business forums.

21

初二 周六

徐家汇天主教堂
Xujiahui Catholic Church

徐汇区蒲西路 158 号
158 Puxi Road, Xuhui District

1910 年 10 月 22 日落成

又称“圣依纳爵堂”，中国著名的天主教堂，清宣统二年(1910)落成，建筑风格为中世纪哥特式，规模宏大，装饰华丽，被誉为“远东第一大教堂”。全国重点文物保护单位。

Officially known as “St. Ignatius Cathedral”, it is a famous Catholic church in China completed in 1910. It is a grand and magnificent Medieval Gothic structure and is honored as the “Greatest Church in the Far East”. It is an important heritage site under state protection.

OCT. 22. 2017 SUNDAY

2017.10

农历丁酉年九月

22

初三　周日

上海大舞台
Shanghai Grand Stage

徐汇区漕溪北路 1111 号
1111 North Caoxi Road, Xuhui District

1999 年 10 月在上体馆基础上改建开放

国内大型的体育馆之一，原名上海体育馆。1999 年保留原体育馆功能的基础上改建。主馆呈圆形，可容纳观众 18000 人。举办过无数经典文艺演出，是上海文化市场繁荣发展的见证地。

Shanghai Grand Stage (formerly named Shanghai Gymnasium), one of domestic large gymnasiums, was renovated on the basis of original gymnasium in 1999. The main circular stadium can accommodate 18,000 audiences. It has held numerous classical art performances and become a beautiful scenery in Shanghai's cultural market.

OCT. 23. 2017 MONDAY　2017.10　农历丁酉年九月

23

初四　周一

霜降

震旦博物馆

Aurora Museum

浦东新区富城路 99 号
99 Fucheng Road, Pudong New Area

2013 年 10 月开馆

坐落于陆家嘴金融区的一家私人博物馆。常设展览以青花瓷器、历代玉器和佛教造像为主。博物馆建筑是建筑大师安藤忠雄在中国第一个完成的改建设计项目。

It is a private museum located in Lujiazui Financial District, and dedicated to the exhibitions of blue-and-white porcelains, jade ware and statues of Buddhism in all ages. The museum building is the first reconstruction project designed and completed by Master Architect Tadao Ando in China.

24

初五 周二

大观园

The Grand View Garden Area

青浦区金泽镇青商公路 701 号
701 Qingshang Highway, Jinze Town, Qingpu District

1988 年 10 月对外开放

根据古典名著《红楼梦》的描写设计而成的大型仿古园林。每年春秋推出红楼艺术节、红楼旅游节等大型表演活动。上海五星级公园、国家 5A 景区。

It is a large antique-looking garden designed according to the descriptions in the classic master piece, Dream of the Red Chamber. Large shows are held in every spring and autumn in the garden, such as the Red Chamber Arts Festival and Red Chamber Tourism Festival. It is a five-star park in Shanghai and one of the 4A-rated national tourist attractions in China.

25

初六 周三

四行仓库

Sihang Warehouse

静安区光复路 1 号
No.1 Guangfu Road, Jing'an District

1937 年 10 月 26 日四行仓库保卫战打响

原是四间银行共同出资建设的仓库，是一座钢筋混凝土结构的六层大厦，2015 年抗战及反法西斯胜利日期间，在原址建成开放了纪念馆，纪念四行仓库保卫战“八百壮士”。

It was originally a warehouse jointly invested by four banks, and a six-storey building of reinforced concrete structure. Now it is a memorial hall built on its original address especially in remembrance of “Eight Hundred Brave Soldiers” who took part in the Defense of Sihang Warehouse during the Battle of Shanghai.

OCT. 26. 2017 THURSDAY *2017.10* 农历丁酉年九月

26

初七　周四

先施公司（东亚饭店）
Sincere Company (East Asia Hotel)

黄浦区南京东路 690 号
690 East Nanjing Road, Huangpu District

1917 年 10 月创立

旧上海四大百货公司之一，也是上海第一家华资现代化大型百货公司。大楼 1917 年建成，其塔楼形象是南京路商业街景观标志之一。市级文物保护单位。

As one of the four major department stores in Shanghai before 1949, Sincere Company is also the first Chinese-owned large modern department store. It was built in 1917, and the image of its tower building is one of the landscape logos on Commercial Street-Nanjing Road. It is a heritage site under municipal protection.

27

初八　周五

金泽镇
Jinze Town

青浦区境域西南
Southwest of Qingpu District

农历九月九重阳节庙会

江南第一桥乡。在上海最大的淡水湖——淀山湖之畔，有“一级空气二级水”之称和“中国最美村镇”之誉。出品市级非物质文化遗产“商榻宣卷”和“商榻阿婆茶”。

Located at the west gate of Shanghai, it abounds with resources, and boasts the largest freshwater lake – Dian Shan Lake reputed as “the most beautiful town in China” for the first-level air and second-level water. The “Shangta Xuanjuan” (art form of rap) and “Grandma’s Tea (Apo Tea) of Shangta” of the town have been listed among intangible cultural heritage at the municipal level.

28

初九　周六

重阳节

秋霞圃

Qiuxia Garden

嘉定区嘉定镇东大街
East Street, Jiading Town, Jiading District

每年 10 月 28 日 –11 月 30 日菊展、盆栽展

具有独特风格的明代园林、上海五大古典园林之最古老者。布局精致、环境幽雅，小巧玲珑，建筑风格小中见大、曲折有致。被誉为中国南方古典园林艺术的翘楚。市级文物保护单位。

It is a garden of the Ming Dynasty with special characteristics and the oldest of the five major classical gardens in Shanghai. With a well-planned layout, tranquil environment, exquisite buildings and perfect arrangements, it is honored as the top of the classical garden art in southern China. It is a heritage site under municipal protection.

OCT. 29. 2017 SUNDAY　2017.10　农历丁酉年九月

29

初十　周日

佘山天文台

Sheshan Observatory

松江区外青松公路 9279 号
9279 Wai Qingsong Highway, Songjiang District

10 月 30 日中国天文日

现代意义上我国最早的天文台、当代中国天文研究中心之一，建于清光绪二十六年（公元 1900 年），积累了大量珍贵的天文资料。全国重点文物保护单位。

It is the earliest modern observatory in China and one of the astronomy research centers in contemporary China. It has accumulated a large amount of precious astronomical data since it was first built in the 26th year under the reign of Emperor Guangxu of the Qing Dynasty (A.D.1900). It is an important heritage site under state protection.

OCT. 30. 2017 MONDAY　　*2017.10*　　农历丁酉年九月

30

十一　周一

长江大桥

Yangtze River Bridge

崇明区长兴岛

Changxing Island, Chongming District

2009 年 10 月 31 日通车

上海到崇明越江通道南隧北桥的重要组成部分之一，全长 16.63 公里，起于隧道长兴岛登陆点，与崇启通道工程相接。大桥设计为双向六车道。

It is a crucial part of the Yangtze River passage which consists of the tunnel in south and the bridge in north from Shanghai to Chongming. With a total length of 16.63 kilometers, it begins at the landing point of the tunnel at Changxing Island, and connects the Chongqi Passage project. It features two-way six-lane road.

OCT. 31. 2017 TUESDAY 2017.10 农历丁酉年九月

31

十二 周二

万圣节

影像·中国
上海地标
2017

拾壹
November
月

宝钢

Baosteel Group Corporation Limited

宝山区
in Baoshan District

改革开放的标志、新中国最大的投资项目，中国最大、最现代化，也是世界级的钢铁联合企业，始建于1978年底。北濒长江，东临吴淞口，厂区面积18.98平方公里。

It is called "Baosteel" for short. It is the largest and the most modern iron and steel company in China, as well as a world-class iron and steel company in the international iron and steel market. The company specializes in manufacturing the steel products of high technological content and high added value.

NOV. 1. 2017 WEDNESDAY 2017.11 农历丁酉年九月

1

十三　周三

福泉山遗址

Fuquan Hill Ancient Cultural Site

青浦区重固镇西

West of Zhonggu Town, Qingpu District

1979 年 11 月 2 日首次开掘

上海的发祥地。距今约五六千年前的新石器时代遗址，有五色土层的文化叠压遗存，被誉为“中国的土建金字塔”、“古上海的历史年表”。全国重点文物保护单位。

Being the “origin of Shanghai”, it is a cultural site of the Neolithic Age about 5,000-6,000 years ago and has the layered cultural relics in five-color soil, honored as the “Clay Pyramid of China” and the “Chronology of Ancient Shanghai”. It is an important heritage site under state protection.

NOV. 2. 2017 THURSDAY　*2017.11*　农历丁酉年九月

2

十四　周四

华严塔

Huayan Pagoda

金山区松隐镇
Songyin Town, Jinshan District

始建于明洪武十三年(1380),为现存浦东、浦南唯一明代古塔。与同方塔、西林塔、礼塔一起为松江府四塔。塔为方形七层,砖木结构,通高32米。市级文物保护单位。

Built in Hongwu Period of the Ming Dynasty (1380), Huayan Pagoda is the sole extant ancient pagoda built in the Ming Dynasty in Pudong and Punan areas of Shanghai.

3

十五　周五

华安大楼（华侨饭店）

Wah On House (Overseas Chinese Hotel)

黄浦区南京西路 104 号
104 West Nanjing Road, Huangpu District

又名华侨饭店、金门饭店，是最早的上海保险业建筑之一、中国人寿保险第一楼。大楼建筑平面呈工字形，外观为新古典主义式。市级文物保护单位。

Also known as Overseas Chinese Hotel and Pacific Hotel, Wah On House is one of Shanghai's oldest insurance buildings and the first floor building of China Life Insurance. It is a historical and cultural site protected at the municipal level.

NOV. 4. 2017 SATURDAY

2017.11

农历丁酉年九月

4

十六　周六

中欧国际工商学院

China Europe International Business School

浦东新区红枫路 699 号
699 Hongfeng Road, Pudong New Area

1994 年由中国政府与欧洲联盟共同创办的世界知名商学院，亚洲有史以来第一个也是目前唯一一个进入《金融时报》世界排名前十的商学院。学院建筑由世界建筑大师贝聿铭设计。

China Europe International Business School is a world's top-ranked business school jointly established by the Chinese government and the European Commission, and also the only one listed among the world's top 10 business colleges by the Financial Times in the history of Asia, ranking the first in Asia for six consecutive years.

NOV. 5. 2017 SUNDAY

2017.11

农历丁酉年九月

5

十七　周日

峻岭公寓（茂名公寓，锦江饭店中、西楼）

Grosvenor House (Maoming Apartment, Jinjiang Hotel Middle, West Building)

黄浦区茂名南路 59 号
59 South Maoming Road, Huangpu District

仿美国现代派风格的高级公寓大楼，始建于 1934 年。建国后称“茂名公寓”。市级文物保护单位。

Renamed Maoming Apartment after 1949, Grosvenor House is a high-grade apartment building imitating American Modernist style, and a number of celebrities have lived here since its completion. It is a historical and cultural site protected at the municipal level.

NOV. 6. 2017 MONDAY

2017.11

农历丁酉年九月

6

十八　周一

徐光启墓

Xu Guangqi's Tomb

徐汇区南丹路光启公园内
inside Guangqi Park, Nandan Road, Xuhui District

1983 年 11 月 8 日徐光启逝世 350 周年开放

明代著名科学家、政治家、中国明代研究和介绍西方科学的先驱徐光启及其妻的墓葬。墓地东有碑廊，刻徐光启画像、传记以及徐光启手稿。全国重点文物保护单位。

It is the tomb of Xu Guangqi — a famous scientist and politician in the Ming Dynasty and a pioneer studying and introducing Western science in the Ming Dynasty of China — and his wife. To the east of the tomb, there is a stone tablet gallery where the portrait, biography and manuscripts of Xu Guangqi are inscribed. It is an important heritage site under state protection.

7

十九　周二

立冬

韬奋故居

Former Residence of Tao Fen

黄浦区重庆南路 205 弄（万宜坊）54 号
54 Lane 205 (Wanyi Fang), South Chongqing Road, Huangpu District

1958 年 11 月 5 日 开放

中国近现代杰出的新闻记者、政论家、出版家，伟大的爱国人士邹韬奋先生 1930–1936 年在上海生活和工作的地方。现辟有纪念馆。市级文物保护单位。

It is where Mr. Zou Taofen, an outstanding journalist, political commentator, and publisher of modern and contemporary China and a great patriot, lived and worked during 1930-1936. Now a memorial hall has been built. It is a heritage site under municipal protection.

NOV. 8. 2017 WEDNESDAY 2017.11 农历丁酉年九月

8

二十 周三

记者节

消防博物馆

Fire Museum

长宁区中山西路 229 号
229 West Zhongshan Road, Changning District

11 月 9 日 中国消防宣传日

国内一流、具有世界先进水平的专业博物馆。2007 年正式开馆，馆藏品包括众多极具史料价值的近代上海消防文物，拥有多功能的消防科技教育体验馆，向公众开展消防教育。

Opened in 2007 officially, Shanghai Fire Museum is a domestic first-class specialized museum of the world's advanced level. Its exhibits include the numerous fire relics with historical values in modern times of Shanghai. It has a multifunctional experience hall of fire science education dedicated to fire education of the public.

9

廿一　周四

上海体育学院

Shanghai University of Sport

杨浦区长海路 345 号
345 Changhai Road, Yangpu District

11 月 10 日校庆

新中国成立后创建最早的体育高等学府。六十多年来，该校为国家培养了一大批高水平竞技体育人才和各类体育专门人才。校行政楼是旧上海市府大楼。

Shanghai University of Sport (SUS), the first university of its kind in the People's Republic of China, was established in November 1952. SUS, formerly known as "East China University of Sport", was under the direct governance of the General Administration of Sport of China and began to be jointly constructed and managed in 2001 by the General Administration of Sport of China and Shanghai Municipal Government.

10

廿二　周五

八仙桥基督教青年会址（淮海饭店）

Yanghwa Bridge YMCA Venue (Huaihai Hotel)

黄浦区西藏南路 123 号

123 South Xizang Road, Huangpu District

11 月 10 日世界青年节

建于 1929 年，上海基督教青年会会所。建筑平面呈凹形，外貌将中国传统的建筑式样融合于西式建筑之中，是“中国色彩的西洋现代建筑”。市级文物保护单位。

Built in 1929, this building is the venue of Shanghai Young Men's Christian Association, a “Western Modern Architecture Chinese Style”. It is a heritage site under municipal protection.

NOV. 11. 2017 SATURDAY

2017.11

农历丁酉年九月

11

廿三　周六

沙逊别墅

Sassoon House (Building 1 Cypress Hotel)

长宁区虹桥路 2419 号
2419 Hongqiao Road, Changning District

20 世纪 30 年代上海最早的外国“冒险家”、房地产大王沙逊的英国乡村风貌别墅，是平面采用不规则布局、外形分割而整体相连的尖顶花园洋房。市级文物保护单位。

Also known as the “Rubicon Garden”, this typical classical English country house is a vacation home built by Sassoon, Shanghai’s first foreign adventurer and real estate magnate in the 1930s. It is a historical and cultural site protected at the municipal level.

NOV. 12. 2017 SUNDAY

2017.11

农历丁酉年九月

12

廿四 周日

史量才旧居

Former Residence of Shi Liangcai

静安区铜仁路 257 号
257 Tongren Road, Jing'an District

1934 年 11 月 13 日史量才遇刺

旧上海报界巨头、《申报》总经理史量才寓所。外围高墙，高三层，有立克壁柱，廊厅宽敞，墙侧有壁炉，廊厅地面、楼梯及扶手米色花纹的大理石。市级文物保护单位。

It is the former residence of Shi Liangcai, a tycoon of newspaperdom and General Manager of Shun Pao in old Shanghai. Enclosed by high walls, the three-storey building features Doric columns, spacious corridor, fireplace in the wall, and beige decorative marble on the floor of corridor, staircase and handle. It is a historical and cultural site protected at the municipal level.

NOV. 13. 2017 MONDAY　　*2017.11*　　农历丁酉年九月

13

廿五　周一

喜马拉雅中心

Zendai Himalayas Center

浦东新区芳甸路 1188 号
No. 1188, Fangdian Road, Pudong New Area

由日籍建筑大师矶崎新设计的当代中国文创商业项目，是一座艺术、生活的体验之城和传播中国艺术、文化、文明的平台。整体由晶莹透亮的立方体和自然质朴的“异型林”构成。

It is a Chinese modern commercial project focusing on culture and innovation. Designed by Japanese master architect Arata Isozaki, it is a building to experience art and life and a platform to spread Chinese arts, culture and civilization. The whole building is composed of transparent and shining cubes along with a simple and natural “abnormal-forest”.

NOV. 14. 2017 TUESDAY　2017.11　农历丁酉年九月

14

廿六　周二

姚氏花园（西郊宾馆 4 号楼）

Yao's Garden (Xijiao Hotel Building 4)

长宁区虹桥路 1921 号
1921 Hongqiao Road, Changning District

建于 1948 年，原系上海水泥厂老板姚有德出资建造，是近代上海很超前的现代建筑。楼前有宽广的大草坪和花园，地形起伏，园内古木参天。市级文物保护单位。

Yao's Garden was built originally with the fund invested by the boss of Shanghai Cement Plant, Yao Youde, in 1948. As a heritage site under municipal protection, it is also a very advanced modern building in Shanghai in Modern China.

NOV. 15. 2017 WEDNESDAY

2017.11

农历丁酉年九月

15

廿七　周三

意大利夜总会
The Italian Nightclub

静安区延安西路 238 号
238 West Yan'an Road, Jing'an District

上世纪 20 年代建成，典型法国文艺复兴时期建筑风格，假 4 层砖混结构，内饰精致，旁有园地和网球场。当时曾为意大利侨在沪夜总会，现为上海市文联所在地。

Completed in the 1920s, the nightclub is of typical French Renaissance style in a fake four-floor brick-masonry structure. It is delicately decorated. It was the nightclub for overseas Italians in Shanghai and now it is the home of Shanghai Federation of Literary and Art Circles.

NOV. 16. 2017 THURSDAY *2017.11* 农历丁酉年九月

16

廿八 周四

泰安路 115 弄花园里弄住宅

Garden Neighborhood Residence at Lane 115 Taian Road

长宁区泰安路 115 弄
Lane 115 Taian Road, Changning District

1948 年由美商德士古洋行为该行高级职员建造的英国古典式和西班牙式假三层住宅。著名历史学家周谷城曾长期居住此弄 6 号。市级文物保护单位。

Built by American Texaco Bank in 1948, it is a fake three-story residence of British classical and Spanish style. The famous historian, Zhou Gucheng had ever lived Lane 6 here for a long time. It is a heritage site under municipal protection.

17

廿九　周五

中国共产党代表团驻沪办事处旧址（周公馆）

CPC Delegation Shanghai Office Memorial Hall (Zhou's Residence)

黄浦区思南路 73 号
73 Sinan Road, Huangpu District

1946 年 11 月 19 日"八办"筹建

抗战胜利后国共谈判期间中共代表团在上海办事机构所在地，又称周公馆。是上海唯一保存完整、对外开放的周恩来纪念地。市级文物保护单位。

It is where the CPC Delegation Shanghai Office was located during the CPC-KMT cooperation period after the Anti-Japanese War and is also called Zhou's Residence. It is the only memorial of Zhou Enlai in Shanghai that is completely preserved and opened to the public. It is a heritage site under municipal protection.

NOV. 18. 2017 SATURDAY

2017.11

农历丁酉年十月

18

初一　周六

寒衣节

南浦大桥

Nanpu Bridge

黄浦区南马路 1410 号
1410 South Horse Road, Huangpu District

1991 年 11 月 19 日通车

落成于 1991 年，上海市区第一座跨越黄浦江的大桥，规模在当今世界同类桥梁中位居第三。主桥为一跨过江的双塔双索面叠合梁结构斜拉桥，桥下可通行 5 万吨级巨轮。

Completed in 1991, it is the first bridge crossing the Huangpu River in Shanghai, ranking the third among the existing similar bridges in the world. The main bridge is a double-pylon, double-plane and superposed-beam structure cable-stayed bridge across the river. The 50,000-tonnage huge ship may pass under the bridge.

19

初二　周日

兴圣教寺塔

Pagoda of Xingshengjiao Temple

松江区中山东路 235 号方塔园内
inside Fang Ta Park, 235 East Zhongshan Road, Songjiang District

中国现存较完整的宋代方型楼阁型木檐砖塔，建于北宋熙宁、元祐年间，俗称“方塔”。该塔大出檐，瘦塔身，被认为是江南造型最美的塔之一。全国重点文物保护单位。

It is a square-style brick pagoda with wooden eaves of the Song Dynasty that is well preserved in China. It is more widely known as “Fang Ta (Square Pagoda)”. It has outreaching eaves and a slim structure, and is considered as one of the most beautiful pagodas of Jiangnan style.

NOV. 20. 2017 MONDAY　　*2017.11*　　农历丁酉年十月

20

初三　周一

8 号桥
No.8 Bridge

黄浦区建国中路 8–10 号
8–10 Middle Jianguo Road, Huangpu District

位于上海建国中路、重庆南路口、北邻上海三大顶级 CBD 之一的淮海路商圈，是由法租界以来老厂房、老仓库改建的特色时尚创意产业园区。现为全国工业旅游示范点。

Located at the intersection of Jianguo Middle Road of Shanghai and South Chongqing Road, and bordering Huaihai Road Business Center - one of Shanghai Top Three CBDs to the north, the No.8 Bridge is a featured fashion and creative industry park rebuilt from the old workshops and warehouses of the French Concession. Now it is the National Industrial Tourist Demonstration Site.

NOV. 21. 2017 TUESDAY　*2017.11*　农历丁酉年十月

21

初四　周二

爱庐

House of Love

静安区东平路 9 号
9 Dongping Road, Jing'an District

蒋介石与宋美龄在上海故居。建于上世纪 30 年代初期，三层砖木结构，四坡法式红瓦屋顶棱角分明，外墙嵌着五彩鹅卵石，典型的法式花园洋房。

The House of Love is the former residence of Chiang Kai-shek and Soong May-ling. It was built in the early 1930s as abrick-wooden structure with three floors. The angular four-slope red-tile roof and the colorful pebbles inlaid in the exter-nalwall make it a typical French style villa.

22

初五 周三

小雪

松江博物馆

Songjiang Museum

松江区中山东路 233 号

233 East Zhongshan Road, Songjiang District

2004 年 11 月 23 日新馆竣工

始建于 1915 年，以征集、收藏、研究、陈列、宣传松江地区历史文化、文物为主，藏品 5000 余件。参观松江博物馆，可追溯上海之根。国家二级博物馆。

With more than 5,000 pieces of collections, Songjiang Museum mainly aims to collect, research, exhibit, and publicize the history, culture, and relics of Songjiang area, from which people can trace back the history of Shanghai. It is a Grade-Two national museum.

23

初六　周四

感恩节

香港广场

Hong Kong Plaza

黄浦区淮海中路 282 号
282 Middle Huaihai Road, Huangpu District

位于淮海中路核心商圈，集办公、购物、娱乐为一体的时尚地标，分为南北两幢高 38 层大楼，以空中走廊连接，全面采用港式管理。

Located in the core business district of Middle Huaihai Road, it is a fashion landmark integrating office, shopping and entertainment. It has two 38-storey buildings connected to each other by an air corridor. It adopts the Hong Kong style management mode.

24

初七　周五

松江唐经幢

Sutra Pillar of the Tang Dynasty in Songjiang

松江区中山东路小学内
inside East Zhongshan Road Primary School, Songjiang District

1964 年 11 月修复完工

建于公元 859 年，是上海现存最古老的建筑物、全国现有唐代经幢中较大者、研究唐代艺术的珍贵实物资料。石灰岩材质，现存 21 级，高 9.3 米。全国重点文物保护单位。

Built in 859, it is the oldest extant structure in Shanghai, a relatively large one among all the existing Buddhism scripture pillars of the Tang Dynasty in China, and a precious material for studying the arts of the Tang Dynasty. It is 9.3 meters high with 21 tiers left. It is an important heritage site under state protection.

NOV. 25. 2017 SATURDAY　　2017.11　　农历丁酉年十月

25

初八　周六

上海音乐学院

Shanghai Conservatory of Music

徐汇区汾阳路 20 号
20 Fenyang Road, Xuhui District

11 月 26 日校庆

我国历史最悠久的高等音乐学府，前身是 1927 年蔡元培等人创办的国立音乐院，被誉为“音乐家的摇篮”。知名校友有贺绿汀、周小燕等。校办公楼原为旅沪犹太人俱乐部。

It is one of the most time-honored higher learning music institutions in the history of China, and has accumulated solid disciplinary foundation in composition, performance and study of classical music. Its predecessor is Shanghai National Training School of Music established by Mr. Tsai Yuen-pei et al. in 1927.

NOV. 26. 2017 SUNDAY

2017.11

农历丁酉年十月

26

初九　周日

万佛阁

Wan Fo Ge (Ten Thousand Buddha Pavilion)

奉贤区奉城北街 189 号
189 North Fengcheng Street, Fengxian District

2003 年 11 月万佛楼落成及万佛开光庆典

上海知名比丘尼道场之一，始建于明朝洪武年间，距今已有六百多年，现存殿宇多为清代所建。大殿的钳状套式梁木结构镶接缜密，堪称古建筑一绝。

It is a Bhiksuni dojo with a relatively large scale in Shanghai. The construction of the pavilion began approximately 600 years ago in Hongwu years of the Ming Dynasty (1368A.D.–1644 A.D.), with most of the remaining halls built in the Qing Dynasty (1644A.D.–1912A.D.). The clamp-like inserted beam structure connects different parts very tightly. It can be regarded as a wonder among ancient buildings.

NOV. 27. 2017 MONDAY

2017.11

农历丁酉年十月

27

初十　周一

醉白池

Zuibaichi (“Drunken Bai Pond”)

松江区人民南路 64 号
64 South Renmin Road, Songjiang District

11 月菊花展

上海五大古典园林之一，也是五大园林中最古老的园林，已有九百余年历史。园内古木葱茏，亭台密布，回廊曲径，古迹甚多，保持着明清江南园林风貌。

Zuibaichi, one of Shanghai's five classical gardens, has a history of more than 900 years, longer than that of the other four gardens. There are lush ancient trees, pavilions and historical sites in the garden. It maintains the style and features of gardens in the south of Yangtze River of the Ming and Qing Dynasties with curved bars and cross sills, winding corridors and devious roads.

28

十一 周二

吴昌硕故居
Former Residence of Wu Changshuo

静安区山西北路 457 弄 12 号
12 Lane 457, North Shanxi Road, Jing'an District

1927 年 11 月 29 日吴昌硕在此逝世

中国美术界海派艺术的创始人、著名画家吴昌硕的最后一处居所。是一幢石库门三间两厢的二层楼房，地处闸北石库门历史文化风貌保护区。市级文物保护单位。

It is the last residence of Wu Changshuo, a famous artist and the founder of Haipai Art in the Chinese arts circle. It is a two-story Shikumen building with three rooms and two wings and located in the Shikumen Historical and Cultural Protection Area of Zhabei. It is a heritage site under municipal protection.

NOV. 29. 2017 WEDNESDAY　*2017.11*　农历丁酉年十月

29

十二　周三

上海戏剧学院
Shanghai Theatre Academy

静安区华山路 630 号
630 Huashan Road, Jing'an District

上海当代戏剧节每年 11 月 –12 月举行

中国著名高等艺术院校。前身为 1945 年由著名戏剧家熊佛西、李健吾等创办上海市立实验戏剧学校。为中国演艺界培养了大批优秀演艺人才，知名校友有黄佐临、余秋雨等。

Founded in 1945, Shanghai Theatre Academy is an art academy of higher learning dedicated to cultivating the art professionals in China. Now it is a municipal university jointly established by Shanghai and the Ministry of Culture. Currently it has three campuses: Huashan Campus, Lianhua Campus and Hongqiao Campus.

NOV. 30. 2017 THURSDAY *2017.11* 农历丁酉年十月

30

十三 周四

影像·中国
上海地标
2017
外白渡桥

拾贰
December
月
Jahwa

和平饭店

Peace Hotel

黄浦区南京东路 20 号
20 Nanjing East Road, Huangpu District

上海第一幢现代派建筑，有“远东第一楼”的美誉，外滩地标。建于 1929 年，芝加哥学派哥特式风格，前身为沙逊大厦内的华懋饭店，巨大的绿色铜护套屋顶为其特色。

It is Shanghai's first modernistic building reputed as No.1 Building in Far East and the landmark of the Bund. With the Gothic style of Chicago school, it was founded in 1929. The predecessor is Cathay Hotel in Sassoon House, featured by the grand green copper-sheathed roof.

1

十四　周五

世界艾滋病日

上海民政博物馆

Shanghai Civil Affairs Museum

黄浦区普育西路 105 号 1 号楼
No.1 Building, 105 West Puyu Road, Huangpu District

2012 年 12 月 2 日对外开放

中国第一家民政博物馆。由序厅、历史文化、业务专题、区县民政、民政英模和民政信息六大板块构成。展示了民国至今的结婚证，居住证，暂住证等，宣传上海民政多年来的公共服务成就。

It is China's first civil affairs museum. Consisting of six parts: the Preface Hall, the History and Culture Exhibition, the Special Professional Work Exhibition and the Civil Affairs Information Exhibition, the museum displays the marriage certificates, residence permits, temporary residence permits, etc. from the Republic of China to present, and publicizes the achievements of Shanghai in civil administration over the years.

DEC. 2. 2017 SATURDAY

2017.12

农历丁酉年十月

2

十五　周六

下元节

四行储蓄会大楼（国际饭店）

Park Hotel

黄浦区南京西路 170 号
170 West Nanjing Road, Huangpu District

1934 年 12 月开业

旧上海由盐业、金城、中南和大陆四大银行组成的四行储蓄会建造的美国装饰艺术派风格的摩天楼，1983 年前是上海制高点，有“东亚第一楼”之称。市级文物保护单位。

Known as the “Tallest Building in the Far East” in the old times, it has kept the record as the tallest building in Shanghai for half a century. It is an important heritage site under state protection, and was awarded as one of the “Top Ten Landmark Hotels with Platinum Award among Chinese and Foreign Hotels”.

DEC. 3. 2017 SUNDAY

2017.12

农历丁酉年十月

3

十六　周日

上海火车站

Shanghai Railway Station

静安区秣陵路 303 号
303 Moling Road, Jing'an District

1916 年 12 月启用

由始建于 1908 年的沪宁铁路上海站改建而成，是全国重要的铁路枢纽、全国铁路客运特等站。与上海南站、上海虹桥站并称上海铁路三大交通枢纽。

Transformed from the Shanghai Station built as early as in 1908, Shanghai Railway Station is the country's major railway hub, and a top class national railway passenger station. It is known as one of the three major transportation hubs of Shanghai, together with Shanghai South Railway Station, and Shanghai Hongqiao Station.

DEC. 4. 2017 MONDAY　　2017.12　　农历丁酉年十月

4

十七　周一

上海科技馆
Shanghai Science & Technology Museum

浦东新区世纪大道 2000 号
2000 Century Avenue, Pudong New Area

2001 年 12 月主馆开放

向公众免费开放的综合性自然科学技术博物馆。馆内各种主题展区和若干个临时展厅，为观众生动演绎“自然、人、科技”的神奇和奥秘。国家 5A 景区。

It is a comprehensive natural science and technology museum that is opened to the public. It consists of various theme exhibition areas and several temporary exhibition halls where the magic and mystery of “nature, mankind and technology” is presented to the visitors in a lively way. It is a 5A-rated national tourist attraction.

5

十八　周二

秀道者塔

Xiudaozhe Pagoda

松江区佘山国家森林公园西佘山

West Sheshan Hill, Sheshan National Forest Park, Songjiang District

1998 年 12 月修缮完工

八角十三层密檐式砖塔，始建于北宋太平天国年间，属于元朝后几乎绝迹的花塔类型。全国重点文物保护单位。

As an octagonal 13-storied brick structure with thick eaves built during Taipingxingguo Period of the Northern Song Dynasty, it is a type of decorated pagoda that was nearly extinct after Yuan Dynasty. It is a municipality protected historic and cultural site.

6

十九　周三

飞行家主题园
The Aviator's Park

浦东新区国展路 311 号
311 Guozhan Road, Pudong New Area

12 月 7 日国际民航日

全国唯一一家以航空文化为传播核心，并外延辐射多个领域的航空文化推广平台，位置在原世博会巴西馆、秘鲁馆、美国馆等场馆，展有拆解后重新组装的波音 747 实体飞机。

The Aviator's Park is the first national themed park focusing on aviation culture communication, and also a platform for promoting aviation culture covering a number of sectors. Located in such venues as Brazil Pavilion, Peru Pavilion and USA Pavilion of the former World Expo, this Park exhibits the real Boeing 747 airplane that is reassembled.

7

二十 周四

大雪

青浦区博物馆

Qingpu District Museum

青浦区华青南路 1000 号
1000 South Huaqing Road, Qingpu District

2004 年 12 月 8 日新馆开馆

青浦地区文物古迹调查、保护、陈列展示的地志性博物馆，藏品近万件。常设陈列“上海古文明之源”和“申城水文化之魅”在全国文博界影响较大。国家二级博物馆。

With nearly ten thousand collections, it is a museum majoring in local history with the task of survey, conservation and exhibition of historic landmarks and sites. It is a Grade-Two national museum.

DEC. 8. 2017 FRIDAY　　*2017.12*　　农历丁酉年十月

8

廿一　周五

龙华革命烈士纪念地

Longhua Revolutionary Martyrs' Cemetery

徐汇区龙华路 2591 号和 2577 号内以及 2501 弄 1 号
Inside 2591 and 2577 Longhua Road, and No.1 Lane 2501, Longhua Road, Xuhui District

1977 年 12 月被公布为上海市纪念地点

由原国民党淞沪警备司令部旧址和龙华革命烈士就义地两部分组成。1985 年国家批准将纪念地和龙华公园合建为龙华烈士陵园。全国重点文物保护单位。

It consists of two parts – the former site of Songhu Garrison Headquarters of the Kuomintang and the place where Longhua revolutionary martyrs sacrificed. In 1985 the memorial and Longhua Park were built, under the approval of the state, into Longhua Martyrs' Cemetery. It is an important heritage site under state protection.

DEC. 9. 2017 SATURDAY

2017.12

农历丁酉年十月

9

廿二　周六

洋山风景区

Yangshan Scenic Spot

上海国际航运中心洋山深水港
Yangshan Deep-water Center, Shanghai International Shipping Center

2005 年 12 月 10 日洋山深水港区一期开港并开放景区

上海国际航运中心洋山深水港的组成部分，也是国家重点风景名胜区嵊泗列岛风景区的一部分。游览景区，可览东海大桥和洋山深水港全貌。

Core region of the Yangshan Deep-water Port of Shanghai International Shipping Center, and also a part of Shengsi Islands Scenic Resort, one of national key scenic spots. Visiting the Yangshan Scenic Spot, people may get a full view of Donghai Bridge and Yangshan Deep-water Port.

DEC. 10. 2017 SUNDAY

2017.12

农历丁酉年十月

10

廿三　周日

港汇广场
Grand Gateway

徐汇区虹桥路 1 号
No.1 Hongqiao Road, Xuhui District

1999 年 12 月开业

位于徐家汇商业中心区域，一座造型独特的上海地标性建筑，由港汇恒隆广场大型购物中心、港汇中心双塔型甲级写字楼、港汇恒隆广场高档涉外酒店式公寓组成。

Located in Shanghai Xujiahui Commercial Centre, it is a landmark complex with unique modeling in Shanghai, and consists of the large shopping mall Grand Gateway 66 Plaza, office buildings Grand Gateway 66 Towers I & II and top grade serviced apartments.

DEC. 11. 2017 MONDAY

2017.12

农历丁酉年十月

11

廿四　周一

马桥遗址

Maqiao Ancient Cultural Relics

闵行区马桥镇俞塘村

Yutang Village, Maqiao Town, Minhang District

1959 年 12 月起发掘

包含唐宋时期、春秋战国时期、商周时期和新石器时 4 个不同时期的古文化遗存。遗址的发现，将上海一带的历史推前了 2000 多年。全国重点文物保护单位。

It contains ancient cultural relics of 4 different ages, including Tang and Song Dynasties, Spring and Autumn and Warring States periods, Shang and Zhou periods, and the Neolithic Age. The discovery of the relics dates back the history of Shanghai by over 2,000 years. It is an important heritage site under state protection.

DEC. 12. 2017 TUESDAY　*2017.12*　农历丁酉年十月

12

廿五　周二

上海海湾国家森林公园
Shanghai Haiwan National Forest Park

奉贤区海湾镇随塘河路 1677 号
1677 Suitanghe Road, Haiwan Town, Fengxian District

占地面积 15983.5 亩，上海最大的人工"绿肺"。以森林为主体，融苗木生产、休闲观光、科学研究和科普教育为一体，再造自然的大型人工城市生态森林公园。国家 4A 景区。

Covering an area of 15,983.5 mus, it is the largest artificial "green lung" of Shanghai. Based on its lush forest, it is a large artificial ecological forest park in a metropolis that focuses on seedling production, leisure & sightseeing, scientific research, and science promotion and education. It is a 4A-rated national tourist attraction.

DEC. 13. 2017 WEDNESDAY　*2017.12*　农历丁酉年十月

13

廿六　周三

海上海

Hi-Shanghai

杨浦区飞虹路 600 弄
Lane 600, Feihong Road, Yangpu District

2006 年 12 月竣工

由住宅、LOFT、商业三大物业形态及海上剧场、海上展馆、海上讲堂三大文化建筑组合而成的创意社区。

Hai Shanghai is an international creative community consisting of residential buildings, LOFT three major property forms, and three cultural buildings, namely Maritime Theatre, Maritime Exhibition Hall and Maritime Lecture Room. It reflects the compatibility and resonance of international cultures in one community.

14

廿七　周四

南汇博物馆

Nanhui Museum

浦东新区惠南镇文师街 18 号

18 Wenshi Street, Huinan Town, Pudong New Area

博物馆分固定展厅和临时展厅。固定展厅分为序厅、上海成陆及浦东古海塘厅、煮海制盐厅、婚嫁迎娶厅、地灵人杰厅五个专题展厅。免费开放。国家三级博物馆。

The Museum is divided into the introduction hall, the room on formation of Shanghai's land and ancient seawall of Pudong area, the room on manufacturing of sea salt, and the room on marriage. It is a Grade-Three national museum.

15

廿八　周五

上海证券交易所
Shanghai Stock Exchange

浦东新区浦东南路 528 号
528 South Pudong Road, Pudong New Area

1990 年 12 月挂牌营业

中国大陆两所证券交易所之一，俗称“主板”。一大批国民经济支柱企业、重点企业、基础行业企业和高新科技企业在此上市。

It is one of the two stock exchanges in Chinese mainland. A large number of the mainstay enterprises, key enterprises, basic industries enterprises and high-tech companies of the national economy have been listed here, and as a result they have not only raised funds for development but also transformed their operational mechanism.

16

廿九 周六

龙美术馆
Long Museum

徐汇区龙腾大道 3398 号、浦东新区罗山路 2255 弄 210 号
3398 Longteng Avenue, Xuhui District; 210 Lane 2255, Luoshan Road, Pudong New Area

目前中国大陆最具规模和收藏实力的私立美术馆。分浦东馆和西岸馆，构成独特的“一城两馆”艺术生态。收藏涵盖中国传统艺术、现当代艺术、“红色经典”艺术，以及亚洲、欧美当代艺术等。

The Long Museum is the largest private art museum with the strongest collection power in China, founded by famous collector Liu Yiqian and his wife Wang Wei. The museum boasts a collection of traditional Chinese arts, contemporary and modern art, “Red Classics” art and contemporary art of Europe and America, etc.

17

三十 周日

上海外国语大学

Shanghai International Studies University

虹口区大连西路 550 号
550 West Dalian Road, Hongkou District

12 月 18 日校庆

新中国第一所高等外语学府，首任校长是著名俄语翻译家、出版家、中国百科全书事业奠基者姜椿芳。松江校区依据不同语种国家的建筑样式设计，充分体现学校多语特色。

Founded in 1949, Shanghai International Studies University is China's first higher education institution in foreign languages after the founding of the People's Republic of China. It is a university jointly founded by the Ministry of Education and Shanghai municipal government, and listed among Project 211 universities.

18

初一 周一

静安寺
Jing'an Temple

静安区南京西路 1686 号
1686 West Nanjing Road, Jing'an District

上海著名的真言宗古刹之一、本市最古老的佛寺之一，可追溯至三国孙吴赤乌年间的沪渎重玄寺。北宋更今名，南宋迁今址，早于上海建城。格局为前寺后塔。市级文物保护单位。

The Jing'an Temple is one of well-known ancient temples of Shingon Buddhism and also one of the oldest temples in Shanghai. It can date back to Hudu Chongxuan Temple in Three Kingdoms period of ancient China. It was renamed in the Northern Song Dynasty and relocated to the present site in the Southern Song Dynasty, earlier than the founding of the city of Shanghai. The layout is designed with the temple in the front and tower in the back.

19

初二　周二

虹桥天街综合体
Hongqiao Sky Street

闵行区申滨南路
South Shenbin Road, Minhang District

上海最大商业综合体，位于虹桥商务区中轴，由7座5A甲级写字楼、体量近25万平方米的天街购物中心、商业街和五星级酒店构成。有空中连廊和地下通道连接虹桥枢纽与国家会展中心。

Located on the axis of Hongqiao CBD, it is the largest commercial complex in Shanghai, composed of seven 5A office buildings, a shopping mall as large as 250,000 square meters, business streets and a five-star hotel. The air gallery and the underground passage connect it with the Hongqiao Hub and the National Convention and Exhibition Center.

DEC. 20. 2017 WEDNESDAY 2017.12 农历丁酉年十一月

20

初三 周三

涌泉坊陈家花园

Chen's Garden at Bubbling Well Lane

静安区愚园路 395 弄
Lane 395 Yuyuan Road, Jing'an District

西班牙式四层建筑，民国时期民族烟草工业三大公司之一的华成烟草公司总经理陈楚湘的住所。花园为仿苏州古典园林，符合当时中西合璧的审美风潮。市级文物保护单位。

This Spanish-style four-story building was built during the period of the Republic of China and the residence of Chen Chuxiang, the general manager of Huacheng Tobacco Company, one of the three national tobacco companies during that period. It is a heritage site under municipal protection.

DEC. 21. 2017 THURSDAY 2017.12 农历丁酉年十一月

21

初四 周四

东林寺

Donglin Temple

金山区朱泾镇东林街 150 号
150 Donglin Street, Zhujing Town, Jinshan District

原名观音堂，始建于元朝至大元年（1308），是上海浦南地区单体建筑面积最大的元、明、清建筑群，寺内有亚洲最大的室内佛像，高约 34 米。国家 4A 景区。

Also called "Guanyin Temple", it was first constructed during the first year of Zhida period of the Yuan Dynasty (1308). It is a complex of structures built in Yuan, Ming and Qing Dynasties with a largest single-building area in the Pu'nan area of Shanghai. In the temple, there is Asia's biggest indoor Budda statue which is about 34 meters high. The temple is a 4A-rated national tourist attraction.

22

初五　周五

冬至

大光明大戏院（大光明电影院）

Grand Theatre (Grand Cinema)

黄浦区南京西路 216 号
216 West Nanjing Road, Huangpu District

1928 年 12 月 23 日京剧大师梅兰芳为戏院开张剪彩

亚洲第一座宽银幕电影院和亚洲第一座立体声电影院，享有“远东第一影院”的盛名，是国内现存最古老的影院之一。市级文物保护单位。

It was Asia's first wide-screen cinema and Asia's first stereo cinema, entitled the "First Theater in the Far East". As a historical and cultural site protected at the municipal level, it is also one of the extant oldest theaters in China now.

DEC. 23. 2017 SATURDAY

2017.12

农历丁酉年十一月

23

初六　周六

欢乐谷
Happy Valley

松江区佘山镇林湖路 888 号
888 Linhu Road, Sheshan Town, Songjiang District

目前国内占地面积最大、游乐设施先进、文化活动丰富的主题公园之一，共有七大主题区、百余项观赏体验项目。国家 4A 景区。

It is one of the theme parks with the largest area, state-of-the-art recreation facilities and rich cultural activities in China. It has seven theme zones and offers over one hundred sightseeing and experience items. It is a 4A-rated national tourist attraction.

DEC. 24. 2017 SUNDAY　　*2017.12*　　农历丁酉年十一月

24

初七　周日

平安夜

国际礼拜堂

International Chapel

徐汇区衡山路 53 号
53 Hengshan Road, Xuhui District

自 1925 年建成始就是上海规模最大的基督教堂，曾以优美的圣乐而斐声沪上。主体建筑为红砖结构仿哥特式教堂。市级文物保护单位。

International Chapel is Shanghai's largest Christian church where many celebrities gave sermons ever since its completion in 1925. It is a historical and cultural site protected at the municipal level.

25

初八　周一

圣诞节

俄罗斯联邦驻上海总领事馆(原苏联领事馆)

Consulate-General of Russian Federation in Shanghai (Former Soviet Union Consulate)

虹口区黄浦路 20 号
20 Huangpu Road, Hongkou District

1991 年 12 月更名

原称"俄罗斯帝国领事馆"、"苏联领事馆"。创设于 1896 年，整体建筑融合巴洛克式和德国复兴时期的风格和元素，与外白渡桥比邻，上海地标景观。市级文物保护单位。

Formerly known as "Russian Empire Consulate" and "Soviet Union Consulate" and renamed in 1991, the Consulate, near the Waibaidu Bridge, is a landmark landscape in Shanghai. It is now also a historical and cultural site protected at the municipal level.

26

初九　周二

田子坊

Tian Zi Fang

黄浦区泰康路 210 弄
Lane 210, Taikang Road, Huangpu District

上海最具影响力的创意产业集聚区之一，以“整旧如旧”的方式，由上海特有的老式石库门建筑群改建而成，来自世界各地的知名艺术家和创意工作室汇集于此，各种特色小店使其更具特色和味道。

It is one of the most influential creative industry cluster areas in Shanghai, rebuilt from the unique Shikumen architectural complex of Shanghai. It gathers famous artists and creative studios from all over the world. And a variety of featured stores make it more distinctive and special.

上海市群众艺术馆

Shanghai Mass Art Center

徐汇区古宜路 125 号
125 Guyi Road, Xuhui District

上海市组织指导群众文化活动，培训群文干部和业余文艺骨干，研究群文艺术的中心。有非遗传习馆、文化讲坛、群文创作、社区文艺指导等功能设施。

Established by the Shanghai Municipal Government, it is a state-owned cultural institution specializing in organizing and guiding cultural activities for the public, training cadres at their posts and amateur backbones of mass culture and art, and researching mass culture and art.

DEC. 29. 2017 FRIDAY　　*2017.12*　　农历丁酉年十一月

29

十二　周五

中国商用飞机浦东基地

The Pudong Base of Commercial Aircraft Corporation of China, Ltd

浦东新区祝桥镇朝晖路 919 号
919 Zhaohui Road, Zhuqiao Town, Podong New Area

2009 年 12 月 28 日奠基

位于浦东国际机场南侧，国内最大、最先进的民用飞机总装制造基地，承担 ARJ21 支线系列、150 座大型客机和双通道大型客机的总装和试飞、交付任务。

Located in the south of Pudong International Airport, it is a large state-owned enterprise and the largest and the most advanced assembly manufacturing base of civil aircraft in China, taking on the tasks of the final assembly, test flight and delivery of ARJ21 series, 150-seat large-type passenger aircraft and twin-aisle large-type passenger aircraft.

27

初十 周三

圆应塔（西林塔）

Yuanying Pagoda (Xilin Pagoda)

松江区中山中路 666 号西林禅寺内
inside Xilin Temple, 666 Middle Zhongshan Road, Songjiang District

原名崇恩宝塔，南宋时为纪念西林禅寺高僧圆应更名，今俗称西林塔，塔身七层八面，高 46.5 米，砖木结构，塔势峥嵘庄严，是上海地区最高的古塔。市级文物保护单位。

Formerly known as Chong'en Pagoda, it was renamed to commemorate the eminent monk Yuanying of Xilin Temple in the South Song Dynasty. Today it is widely known as Xilin Pagoda. The pagoda is a brick-wooden structure, 46.5 meters in height, with seven stories and eight facets. It is the tallest ancient pagoda in Shanghai and a heritage site under municipal protection.

DEC. 28. 2017 THURSDAY　　2017.12　　农历丁酉年十一月

28

十一　周四

30

十三 周六

新天地

Xintiandi

黄浦区太仓路 181 弄
Lane 181, Taicang Road, Huangpu District

以上海独特的石库门建筑旧区为基础改造成的集餐饮、商业、娱乐、文化的休闲步行街。中西融合、新旧结合的基调和风格，让海内外游客品味独特的海派文化。

With multiple functions of catering, commerce, entertainment and culture,Xintiandi is a stylish pedestrian street renovated based on an old district of Shikumen buildings—a unique architectural style of Shanghai.Its integration of the Chinese and western elementsas well as the modern and antique stylesallows local and overseas visitors to have a tasteof the unique Shanghai culture.

DEC. 31. 2017 SUNDAY 2017.12 农历丁酉年十一月

31

十四 周日

图书在版编目（CIP）数据
上海地标. 2017 / 《影像中国》编辑部编.
— 上海:东方出版中心, 2016.11
（影像中国）
ISBN 978-7-5473-1028-1
Ⅰ. ①上… Ⅱ. ①影… Ⅲ. ①上海—概况 Ⅳ.
①K925.1
中国版本图书馆CIP数据核字(2016)第245316号

总 策 划: 李智平
主 编: 王祖光
编辑部主任: 黄 客
编辑部成员: 董旖旎 李 娜 林 倩 董沁妍
摄 影: 陈海汶 李 燕 杨晓喆 赵晓斌等
封面剪纸: 奚小琴
定 制: 上海众响信息技术有限公司
责任编辑: 丁国生
支持机构: 上海市文化创意产业推进领导小组办公室

上海地标. 2017
出版发行：中国出版集团 东方出版中心
地 址：上海市仙霞路345 号
电 话：021-62417400
邮政编码：200336
经 销：全国新华书店
印 刷：上海雅昌艺术印刷有限公司
开 本：889×1194毫米 1/48
印 张：16
版 次：2016 年11月第1 版第1次印刷
ISBN 978-7-5473-1028-1
定 价：128.00元

版权所有，侵权必究
东方出版中心邮购部 电话：021-62597143

26

初九 周二

田子坊
Tian Zi Fang

黄浦区泰康路 210 弄
Lane 210, Taikang Road, Huangpu District

上海最具影响力的创意产业集聚区之一，以“整旧如旧”的方式，由上海特有的老式石库门建筑群改建而成，来自世界各地的知名艺术家和创意工作室汇集于此，各种特色小店使其更具特色和味道。

It is one of the most influential creative industry cluster areas in Shanghai, rebuilt from the unique Shikumen architectural complex of Shanghai. It gathers famous artists and creative studios from all over the world. And a variety of featured stores make it more distinctive and special.

战略伙伴：

大佳网

上海市文创办

东方财富网

图游

TOP2010

上海中版翻译